The Killing Of...
PARADISE PLANET

Secrets of that forgotten world
BEFORE the great disaster

Book 1 of a trilogy

TEACH Services, Inc.
www.TEACHServices.com

2008 09 10 11 12 13 14 · 5 4 3 2 1

Published by

TEACH Services, Inc.
www.TEACHServices.com

About the author

Jonathan Gray has travelled the world to gather data
on ancient mysteries. A serious student of pre-history,
he has investigated numerous archaeological sites, and
has also penetrated some largely un-explored areas,
including parts of the Amazon headwaters.

Other books by Jonathan Gray

Dead Men's Secrets
Sting of the Scorpion
The Ark Conspiracy
Curse of the Hatana Gods
64 Secrets Ahead of Us
Bizarre Origin of Egypt's Ancient Gods
The Lost World of Giants
Discoveries: Questions Answered
Sinai's Exciting Secrets
Ark of the Covenant
Surprise Witness
The Corpse Came Back
The Discovery That's Toppling Evolution
UFO Aliens: The Deadly Secret
Jesus Christ – Fact or Fake?
The Da Vinci Fraud

CONTENTS

PREFACE

It was Black November. Two billion or more people, with their astonishing technology, *vanished from the face of the earth.* This lost super race beat us to the moon, computers and nuclear war.

In that popular book *Dead Men's Secrets,* Jonathan Gray uncovered some startling information about this super civilisation that was wiped out in a cosmic disaster.

More astonishing discoveries continue to surface and confirm the basic thesis of that book.

It is now time to take a very close look at *the big event itself...* the disaster that minced to atoms that advanced world.

This is not intended to be a detailed reference work, but a simple, straight-forward explanation of the main factors involved. For the reader who wants to dig deeper, there is an abundance of further information available.

But first a note concerning the date of that event. When *Dead Men's Secrets* was released, the author was prepared to go along with the common estimate that the post-Flood civilisations of Egypt, Sumeria, etcetra, sprang up suddenly around 3000 B.C.

Nevertheless, it was felt necessary to state [1] that "the precise *time...* may be subject to revision." That prediction has proven justified. New research requires that the date of the Deluge be revised closer to our time, to 2345 B.C. Numerous and varied methods support this revision.[2]

As a consequence, the rapid post-Flood rise of the new civilisations would require similar adjustment.

Dates from c.2250 onward are not affected. The date of the Babel world government collapse is as solid as ever. It will be seen, however, that there is a considerable shortening of history between the Deluge disaster and the Babel episode.

The estimated number of active volcanoes at that time should also be changed - drastically increased, in fact.

It will be noted that the above adjustments are in the realm of numbers, not in the facts themselves.

Welcome to a new adventure in discovery.

PROLOGUE

"Porrett is coming out of his apartment... GET READY."

"The wind's wild. ...It's gonna be hard to hit him!"

"This is our only chance. DON'T MISS! ...NOW!"

A fast aim... skidding tyres... CRASH...

"Let's get outta here!"

George Porrett struggled to his feet, flicking off the mud. "Boy, was that close!" he thought. "They missed me again." He glanced upward. Somehow Porrett felt protected. 'THANK YOU," he breathed.

"...Hello, George. You're looking shaken. Come in. Come in. ...What is it?"

"There's been another attempt on my life."

"Just a minute. Betty, call Ray and Ken. Get them in right away."

"...It's open warfare, guys. These photographs are hot. This whole discovery. They're out to silence us..."

Much of the data had been known for a while. But now it threatened to blow sky-high some reputations. Careers and big money were at stake. All very upsetting. One or two persons were getting so strung up about it, they would do anything. Yes, even kill.

This book is about LIFE and DEATH, LOVE and HATE. The big stuff. It's about *THAT* discovery - a haunting secret from our past.

You might wonder how the distant past could ever arouse men to threaten each other now. But, as you read on, you may understand why some people currently consider this so important.

Briefly, this is the discovery...

DISCOVERED –

- Buried alive! **From Australia to Alaska: billions of corpses of animals and people.**
- Violently mixed: **large animals of DEEP sea and land, TOGETHER!**
- **Elephants and** tropical **palm trees: SUDDENLY entombed** in ice.

TODAY our earth is spoiled and mostly uninhabitable. But this was not always so.

THERE WAS A TIME when everything lived under a giant, protective canopy. The atmosphere was temperature-controlled. It was a paradise planet.

THEN SOMETHING HAPPENED
It was sudden. A whole world vanished. This sudden disappearance is like a mystery thriller with the last pages torn out... except that...

THERE ARE ALSO
Legends – racial traditions –that speak of such an event. And they recall what really happened.

BUT THE REAL SHOCKER
Is the physical evidence. **The killing of a whole planet is the** most astonishing true story you'll ever hear.

FACT... MYSTERY... ADVENTURE...

In *Dead Men's Secrets*, an investigation was made into lost cities of the dead and the surprising discoveries they held. We explored our planet's jungles, desert sands and seafloor to extract forgotten secrets

10

of a technology that had vanished. There emerged tantalising hints of a lost super race that had been wiped out in some cosmic disaster.

Now it's time to peer closer into that mysterious lost world. We shall discover the event that snuffed it out. And its impact on those who survived and on their descendants. Indeed, as we shall find, shock waves from this event are still being felt today. Dead men will talk to us. Make no mistake. The implications are dynamite.

Nevertheless, our quest is not based on ancient texts and reports, but on accepted scientific discoveries. There are recently discovered objects that cannot be dismissed - namely artefacts and corpses, entombed in the violently damaged structure of the earth's crust. Some are in museums. These speak in thundertones of a disaster which was sudden and total.

Stand by for adventure... - gigantic adventure.

Come with me now, far back into the centre of the Great Unknown. Our destination: a strange planet (albeit our own), 5,000 years in the past.

We shall look in upon *this super world that vanished so completely we thought it never existed.*

Let's begin.

1

Sudden change -

CITY UNDER THE SEA

"It's too bizarre!"

I stared at Doug. Was he nuts?

"But it's true," he repeated. "He was found here. Poor thing. Had no chance. Whatever happened, it was all so sudden. He was snap-frozen." Doug cracked his knuckles. "...just like that!

"Didn't even have time to swallow. When they found him, the fresh-chewed veges were still on his tongue. Fresh food in his stomach... still there, undigested.

"And here - fresh, ripe plums, still on the branches. Snap frozen, I tell you. Then suddenly buried beneath hundreds of feet of muck.

"And over here..."

I caught Doug's excitement. Bent over the map, jumping from place to place, he pointed out the spots.

Now he was in Alaska, now in Siberia... Antarctica too.

'BUT THEY'RE TROPICAL'" I protested. "What are *tropical* animals and plants doing *frozen in ice*?"

"Not ice," corrected Doug. "It's FROZEN water-laid muck."

Yes, it was all so bizarre. But true! There was the evidence! What could have happened so suddenly that day long ago?

It was time to find out...

A SUDDEN CHANGE: PHYSICAL EVIDENCE

As my investigation proceeded, it soon became clear that there was evidence for an ancient globally warm climate - from pole to pole. That itself was astonishing enough. But the next discovery was to be no less startling.

It must have changed SUDDENLY. So suddenly that tropical animals were snap-frozen in mid-motion, to be preserved to this day with undigested food in their stomachs!

Something *deadly and very sudden* wiped out the population, changed the climate, and REVERSED the land and water distribution of this planet.

Did you get that? I'll repeat it.

There is evidence that our planet - this planet Earth of ours - was once subtropical from pole to pole and that - believe it or not - the SEA LEVEL stood 2 or 3 miles LOWER than now.

There is evidence that *something deadly and very SUDDEN* changed the climate in a flash, reversed the land and water distribution of the globe and virtually wiped out the world's population.

Yes, I know somebody will say I'm off my rocker. But before you do, let me state that *THERE IS PERSUASIVE EVIDENCE THAT THE WORLD WAS ONCE VASTLY DIFFERENT.*

And compelling also is the evidence that *WHATEVER CHANGED IT OCCURRED SUDDENLY.*

A DAMAGED PLANET

In fact, I have rarely investigated anything I thought was more factual.

I am now convinced that not so long ago there occurred a watery catastrophe of such magnitude that the earth is still reeling from its onslaught.

This global deluge explains why today's world is far from perfect. We inhabit a planet that has been DAMAGED and IMPOVERISHED, still suffering the effects of a worldwide disaster.

You will notice from the graph below that *water* covers almost three quarters of our planet's surface.

Of the 30 percent area that is land, less than half is suitable for habitation at present. In other words, only 18 percent of our planet's surface is now suitable for human habitation.

Large areas now under perpetual desert or ice were once lush, fertile and inhabited. Large areas now under the sea were likewise habitable. I shall give you evidence of this.

Then something happened suddenly. It changed everything.

Yes, we are now living on a planet that is DAMAGED and IMPOVERISHED.

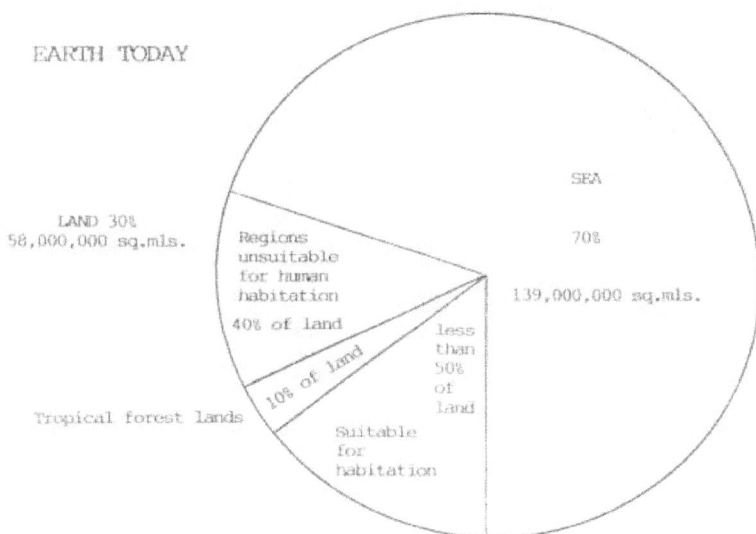

EARTH TODAY

LAND 30%
58,000,000 sq.mls.

SEA

70%

139,000,000 sq.mls.

Regions
unsuitable
for human
habitation
40% of land

10% of land

less
than
50%
of
land

Tropical forest lands

Suitable
for
habitation

But this is not all. The earth after the Disaster was not only considerably reduced in land area. But even in this SHRUNKEN land surface area, the fertility of the soil and the natural resources necessary for human progress are UNEQUALLY distributed and LARGELY BURIED.

But this was not so before the Great Flood. There! I've said it. I've said something that is anathema to the established theory of world history. I've mentioned the GREAT FLOOD.

DROWNED LAND

The Hitler war was now three years in the past. The Swedish research ship "Albatross" had just returned from a peaceful reconnaissance in the South Atlantic.

Had you peeped through a lattice window in a little house outside Stockholm, you might have seen two men, one of them bearded, huddled across a table, engaged in lively talk.

One of them, in fact, looked almost wild-eyed. But, knowing him as a well-balanced, sober man, you would have to admit that whatever it was that now had him so excited must be something extraordinary.

15

"I swear to you, it's incredible! Do you know, we were sounding the seabed 700 miles east of Brazil. And we brought up core samples of *fresh-water plants*! Can you believe that! And do you know how deep they were? *Three thousand metres*! These samples actually contained micro-organisms, twigs, plants and even tree bark."

The speaker was Professor Hans Pettersson, who had led the expedition.

"I cannot explain it - except that that land must have sunk on the spot."

ANOTHER DISCOVERY

Within a similar time frame, discussion was hot in London. *Coral* had been recovered from depths of over 3,000 feet (1,000 metres) in mid-Atlantic Ocean sites. Now we all know that coral grows only close to sea level.

So in London, England, someone else was making a chilling diagnosis:

"Either the seabed dropped thousands of feet or the sea rose mightily."

AND STILL ANOTHER

Meanwhile, at Columbia University in the U.S.A., Professor Maurice Ewing, a prominent marine geologist, was reporting on an expedition that had descended to submerged plateaus at a depth of 5,000 feet.

He was being interrogated. "Tell us, what did you find?"

"It's quite amazing," was his response. "At five thousand feet down, the expeditioners discovered prehistoric *beach sand*. It was brought up in one case from a depth of two miles and the other nearly three and one half miles, far from any place where beaches exist today."

"How far from land was this?"

"One deposit was 1,200 miles from the nearest land."

As we all know, sandy beaches form from waves breaking on the edge of the coastal rim of the seas. Beach sand does not form deep down on the ocean bottom.

Then Dr. Ewing dropped his bombshell: "Either the land must have sunk two or three miles or the sea must have been two or three miles lower than now. Either conclusion is startling." [1]

WHAT THIS MEANS

These facts can be interpreted in only two ways: either there was a mighty ocean bed *subsidence* (unexplainable by orthodox science), *or* a huge (likewise unexplained) *addition of water* to the ocean.

Let's briefly consider these.

1. **Sudden subsidence**

Otto Muck draws attention to the sharp, fine profiles of much of the landscape that is now drowned by the ocean. He notes:

"The sharp, fine profiles would have been eroded, and the lava covering the ocean floor would have decayed if all this rocky terrain had been immersed in sea water for more than 15,000 years. Chemical forces are very destructive, but mechanical forces are equally so. Sharp edges and points can be ground down and blunted by abrasion, erosion, and the action of waves. But the entire seabed below the present surf zone has retained its sharpness of profile. *Had the subsidence taken place gradually*, chemical and other forces would have ground down this sharp profile within a few hundred years." [2]

If the land had sunk slowly, even the surf would have worn away these profiles. No, it was a *rapid* subsidence, if a subsidence it was.

This *sudden* collapse of an area covering many millions of square miles must have been accompanied by violent seismic and volcanic activity. The evidence does not support a gradual sinking, but rather a cataclysmic event.

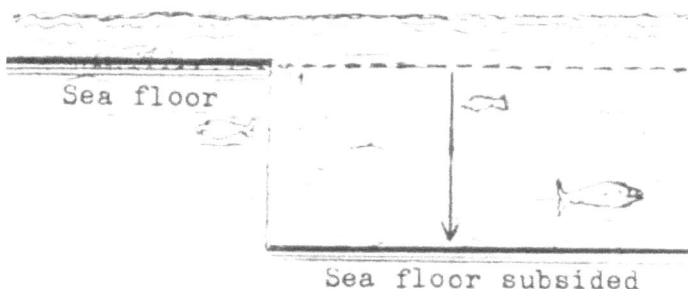

Such subsidence is perfectly in keeping with the centuries-long adjustments that occurred after the Great Flood trauma. These will be explained in detail in the third book of this series.

2.   Pre-Flood sea level lower

However, some of the data strongly suggest that the sea level actually was several thousand feet lower than at present - that there was LESS WATER in the ocean at one time. These discoveries suggest that we are uncovering evidence of a former sea level!

But this would call for a relatively sudden increase of 30 percent in the volume of the ocean. The compelling question is, WHERE DID THIS WATER COME FROM? Few geologists can bring themselves to answer this.

Obviously, melting ice sheets could never have contained enough water to raise the ocean level *thousands* of feet. So we can forget melting ice sheets being the cause.

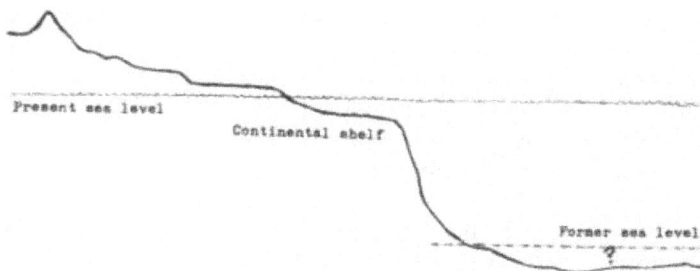

CITY ON THE SEABED?

Now for another surprise. This time the excitement was in the Pacific. The year was 1965. A research vessel named "Anton Brunn" was investigating the Nazca Trench, off Peru.

The sonar operator called for the captain.

"I don't know what to make of this," he murmured. "Around here, the ocean floor is all mud bottom. But just take in these sonar recordings... unusual shapes on the ocean floor! I'm puzzled."

"Better lower a camera," came the order.

At a depth of 6,000 feet a photograph revealed huge *upright pillars and walls*, some of which seemed to have *writing* on them. In other nearby locations, apparently artificially shaped stones lay on their sides, as though they had toppled over.

The crew rubbed their eyes and kept staring. Could this really be? ...the remains of a city under a mass of water more than a mile deep!

Was this a city that had been overwhelmed suddenly by some gigantic disaster? And now it was buried under 6,000 feet (2,000 metres) of ocean?

Water which never went away.

...Thus begins our investigation of a lost world - one which was like a paradise, in many ways. It was different beyond our wildest dreams. Yet it was a REAL WORLD. As real as ours.

In the next three chapters we shall probe its treasures, peer into its mysteries and uncover a few of its tantalising secrets. Are you ready? Let's sneak back in time...

A SUDDEN CHANGE - Summary

A ONCE DIFFERENT WORLD   There is evidence that our planet was once subtropical from pole to pole. Moreover, there was more land - and the sea level stood 2 or 3 miles lower than now.

A DAMAGED PLANET TODAY   We now inhabit a world that is damaged and impoverished, still suffering the effects of some worldwide disaster.

A SUDDEN CHANGE OCCURRED   There is evidence that something deadly and very sudden changed the climate in a flash, reversed the land and water ratio and virtually wiped out the world's population.

REMAINS UNDER THE SEA   Some intriguing finds on the seabed testify to this sudden change that interrupted human history.

2

The first world (a) -

ANTARCTICA'S PALM BEACHES

"Can you believe it!" shouted Giselle. "Look, look! There's a water-skiier!"

"Can't be!" I retorted.

"Yes, yes, look!"

The very word "water-skiier" was enough to awaken a stampede. Everyone crammed against the starboard windows. Our plane dipped down to a thousand feet. Sure enough, behind a powerboat, on a small stretch of water skimmed some guy in a wet suit.

"It's minus sixty out there!" someone exclaimed.

There was good reason for the fuss. This was Antarctica, you see. Just down the coast a 200 mile-per-hour blizzard was raging, whipping up a deadly ice cloud. But here, in frozen sunshine, skiied a Frenchman.

I recalled with amusement that some years ago the French government had passed a law for its Adelie Land territory in Antarctica, exempting its inhabitants from military service - when its only inhabitants were penguins!

Emperor penguins…exempt from military service!
(picture: *Junior World Encyclopedia*)

Now Antarctica had a French research base. And we knew, dropping out of the sky unannounced, that we were their first visual contact with the outside world in six months.

Antarctica... Between the stark white ice cliffs and the black of the ocean below us appeared a ribbon of milky blue, where the ice plunged under the water. It was so beautiful, I just gasped.

Yet it is a bleak and deadly land. That water-skiier could not dry off under a tropical palm.

Not any more.

A WORLDWIDE WARM CLIMATE

There is definite evidence that our planet once presented a warm subtropical climate from pole to pole.

- *Corals*, which grow only in warm waters (of at least 20 degrees Centigrade) once grew near the poles. Canada, Alaska, Newfoundland, Greenland and Spitzbergen contain fossil coral.
- *Coal seams* are also found near the poles. The vast coal beds are simply fossilised remains of trees and plants.
- The remains of *animals* now confined to warm regions are found all over the earth.

Vegetation and animals

- Antarctica: In 1976, an Italian expedition discovered away below the ice - a petrified forest!
- Antarctica: The Admiral Byrd expedition found and photographed a mountain composed totally of coal, indicating former lush growth here. They also found ancient palm trees under the ice.
- Antarctica: In 1968, in the mountains of central Antarctica, an American expedition came upon the jaw bone of a crocodile-like amphibian (called a labyrinthodont), as well as skeletons of other animals - creatures that could have survived only in a warm to hot climate. Similar finds were made again in 1986.
- Northern polar regions: Abundant remains of tropical animals have been uncovered in icy Greenland, Alaska and Siberia.
- In these same northern polar regions are numerous fossil trees: beech, myrtle, laurel, breadfruit, cinnamen, oak, walnut, banana, grape vines, and so on. And from a line north of Labrador across to Alaska: giant sequoias.
- Spitzbergen and Greenland now shiver in darkness for half of the year and lie almost continuously under snow and ice. Yet a rich, temperate *flora* once covered these icy wastes in the Arctic Ocean. Fossil remains of magnolias, fig trees, palms, arborescent ferns (which are typically tropical) and *animals* from warm climates have been discovered... also pines, firs, spruces, cypresses, elms, hazels and water lilies.
- South polar region: Redwood forests are found buried under massive ice deposits. These towering giants (now typically found in the north-west of the U.S.A.) once flourished in many diverse parts of the world, as evidenced by many coal and fossil finds.
- Back to the Arctic Circle: Here are two very interesting island groups - the New Siberian Islands and the Spitzbergen Islands. Remarkable things have been reported by explorers who have been there. Immense frozen gravel mounts were discovered to have entombed within them *entire fruit trees with the fruit still on them.* [1]

- In the New Siberian Islands, whole palm trees have been found, with their leaves and fruit.

Dennis R. Petersen

Tropical animals cannot live in icy water. Neither can sub-tropical plants ripen seeds and sow themselves in arctic conditions.

ONE CLIMATE WORLDWIDE

Geologist George McCready Price sums up the findings:

"If we listen to the unequivocal testimony of tropical plants and animals found away to the north and even within the arctic regions, we must declare that *geology knows only one climate* until this **sudden change** came;   and this astonishing climate seems to have been practically uniform *over the entire globe.*" [2]

Others concur:

"There is but one climate known to the ancient fossil world as revealed by the plants and animals entombed in the rocks, and the climate was a mantle of *springlike loveliness* which seems to have prevailed continuously *over the whole globe.*   Just *how* the world could have thus been warmed all over may be a matter of conjecture; *that it was* so warmed effectively and continuously is a matter of fact." [3]

"When nearly the same plants are found in Greenland and Guinea; when the same species, now extinct, are met with of equal development at the equator as at the pole, we cannot but admit that at this period *the temperature of the globe was nearly alike everywhere.*

"What we now call climate was unknown in these geological times. There seems to have been then only one climate *over the whole globe.*" [4]

Paleobotanist R.W. Chaney has shown from fossil plants that the climate was slightly warmer near the equator and cooler near the poles. [5] There were these slight differences of latitude climate, but not the present zonal extremes. Overall, the climate of Planet Earth was mild and springlike, perfect from pole to pole.

This same warm global climate
IN ALL SO-CALLED "AGES" OF STRATA

Worldwide warm climate seems to be indicated in practically every so-called "age" of rock strata. This is generally acknowledged. Whitcomb and Morris, in *The Genesis Flood*, cite testimony to this universally mild and warm climate in the subdivision rocks of the Proterozoic (Azoic), Paleozoic, Mesozoic and Cenozoic "periods" - that is, in practically all the strata [6] Basically all of these strata contain the buried life of the ancient world.

To many geologists this is perplexing.

For example, von Engeln and Caster say concerning the Jurassic system:

"This universal tropicality is difficult to explain." [7]

THIS ANCIENT WORLD EXISTED
WITHIN THE MEMORY OF MANKIND

There is good reason to believe that this world of perfect climate existed within the memory of the human race.

The traditions of ancient humanity preserve the recollection of it.

The ancient Chinese say that before the great Catastrophe, "four seasons succeeded each other regularly and without confusion. There were no impetuous winds, nor excessive rains. The sun and moon, without ever being clouded, furnished a light purer and brighter than now." [8]

Numerous ancient traditions contain details of the world "before the Flood", details which seem to stem from a common origin: the original perfect state; a glorious land; long age spans; but growing disobedience to spiritual laws - and eventual destruction.

A VERY DIFFERENT WORLD

There is evidence that the entire earth was VERY DIFFERENT FROM THAT WHICH WE NOW EXPERIENCE. It was a fabulous world beyond our power to imagine, much less to describe.

There were no ice caps, no blizzards or rigors of arctic cold, no disease-breeding heat of the tropics.

There were no enormous wastelands. No deserts, barren patches, or bleak and sterile hills. The rocky features were hidden, everywhere covered with a mantle of fertile soil.

Mountains

The mountain ranges were not the same high, forbidding walls as found in the world of today. They were much lower, covered with vegetation, and did not seriously interfere with the climate as do today's mountains.

As E.H. Colbert noted in *Scientific Monthly*:

"The land was low and there were no high mountains forming physical or climatic barriers." [9]

Ocean beds

Conversely, the ocean beds were relatively shallower than now.

Land distribution

There is evidence that the land and water areas were more evenly distributed, with more land than water, perhaps very much more. The great ocean basins of today did not exist. Instead, the land was partitioned by narrow seas and possibly shallow epi-continental seas (or marshes) in some regions of the earth.

Have you noticed on maps how many of the contours of the continental shores seem to fit like so many parts of a big puzzle? The distribution of fossils indicates that the present continental masses were once joined.

Map: Glenn R. Morton, after Kirillov, I., 1958, in Expanding Earth Symposium, p.22

This has led to the idea among many scientists of "continental drift" - something speculated to have occurred over millions of years.

But could it just as well have happened suddenly through some massive upheaval of our earth?

Today the study of the ocean floor confirms that the land masses HAVE been RIPPED apart.

Yes, there used to be ONE continental land mass.

The western continental shelf of Africa is believed to have fitted like a jigsaw piece into South America's eastern side. However, the small amount of erosion of these matching lines suggests not millions of years, but a fairly *recent* ripping apart.

Up to this point, we have considered only solid proven FACTS - facts that can be physically examined. Such as those from which we deduce a former ONE continental land mass, for example.

But here, I shall introduce an ancient document. Would it surprise you to learn that world history as given in the biblical book of Genesis agrees with this? Originally, so the record goes, "the waters were gathered into ONE place" in contrast to the "dry land." [10]

Perhaps there is some truth in its "myths", after all!

As we advance into our discovery of known FACTS concerning the lost "paradise" world and what caused it to vanish, I believe we shall see increasing evidence that this often scorned book of Genesis does indeed contain forgotten knowledge of the past.

Without apology, therefore I shall occasionally mention its references to that vanished world.

Watering system

Genesis tells us that one central river system branched into four rivers which extended and encircled areas of land. [11]

At least five "pre-Flood" regions are identified - Eden, Havilah, Cush, Asshur and Nod.

(Speculation is futile regarding the site of Eden's famous "garden"; the upheaval that changed the first world was thorough.)

In those days no part of the land was too far from water; thus warm water currents were able to contribute to a mild climate everywhere. There was less range between highs and lows.

Extensive underground waterways served as a subirrigation system. The warm waters below the earth's crust emerged through great artesian springs to feed the surface rivers. (In Genesis 7:11 these are called "the fountains of the great deep".)

Remains of these subterranean streams have been discovered. We call them geosynclines.

No winds, storms or rain

We have noted the uniformly warm temperatures and the much gentler topography of this original world.

Winds and storms would have been impossible, since these result basically from interchange between hot and cold atmospheric conditions.

Cyclonic winds did not occur, but there was, by implication, the presence of gentle breezes.

The great global air mass movements that sustain the present hydrological cycle would have been impossible. Heavy rains could never have occurred.

Thus one can take seriously the statement in Genesis [12] that daily local evaporation and transpiration, with evening cooling and condensation, produced a daily mist. This would have kept the earth everywhere in a comfortable state of humidity and provided ample moisture to sustain lush life everywhere. There was no need for rain.

The warm waters of the narrow, shallow sea network likewise sustained a thriving complex of marine life all over the world.

This primeval planet was indeed "very good." [13]

Lush vegetation and animal life

The luxuriance of vegetation must have been a delight to the eyes. It was more lush than we have ever seen - and that everywhere.

How often today do we travel through tired, dry areas of stunted plants, which seem to frantically clutch at every available drop of water! And is it not a relief to arrive home and rest our delighted eyes on the fresh greenness of a tended garden?

Originally the whole earth was a fresh landscape of vegetation springing up easily under optimum conditions. For example, in Antarctica, as we have noted, are fossil remains of tropical and temperate trees, giant ferns, and imprints of grasses, as well as vast layers of coal, extending almost to the South Pole itself; also tropical animals.

Today's enormous coal beds worldwide are irrefutable proof of the unparalleled luxuriance of plant life in the old world.

3

The first world (b) -

THE WEATHER MAN
WHO GOT IT WRONG!

"Well, viewers," beamed the T.V. weather man, sheepishly, "tonight I really must apologise to you.

"In last night's forecast I told you to water your gardens. And to expect fine weather for the next four days. Well I don't have to tell you that I went home and had just finished watering my garden when it simply poured down!"

I smiled. This was Adelaide, Australia. But that story could have happened anywhere.

So much for our weather forecasting technology. With all our sophisticated predictions, we can still say... "Surprise!"

No such luck if you were a weather forecaster 5,000 years ago. There were no surprises. The weather was as predictable as the rising of the sun.

So you could never get yourself a job as a weather man, nor as a weather girl, no matter how charming you might be. That job just never existed... anywhere on earth.

Everyone knew what the weather would be like... tomorrow, next week, next month, and twenty months from now. It never changed. Never any rain. No thunderstoirms, no hurricanes, no droughts, no floods. If you offered your services to the T.V. station, they'd laugh you out of town!

Yes, we're talking about this planet earth of ours.

How things have changed!

Before the Great Disaster, this was a protected planet.

LIVING UNDER THE DOME

It is quite possible that the earth was at that time surrounded by an outer water canopy which intercepted the direct rays of the sun.

31

Genesis speaks of the "waters *above* the firmament." [1]   The Hebrew word translated "firmament" means, literally, "expanse", referring to the atmosphere, or at least the troposphere (which is that part of the atmosphere in which there are no convection currents, storms, clouds, etc, - below the stratosphere).

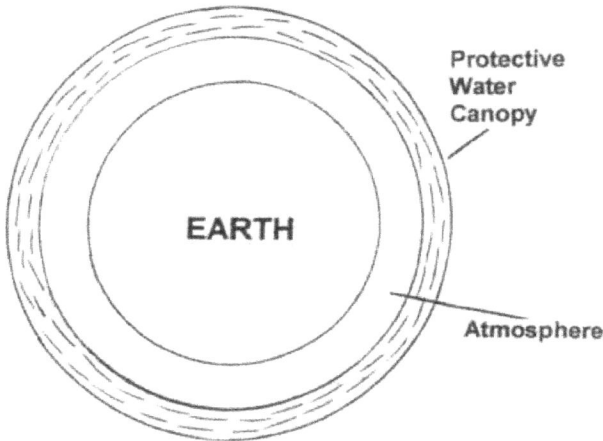

Can such a phenomenon really exist? Indeed. Canopies are quite common around the planets of our solar system. The planets Venus and Jupiter, and also Saturn's moon, Titan, each have vapour or cloud canopies completely surrounding them.

Such a canopy would diffuse the sun's rays all over the globe. It would give the world a uniform climate. Incoming solar heat would diffuse so equally over all zones, that a subtropical climate would prevail from pole to pole.

The conditions would be like those in a *terrarium*! The average temperature would be about 72 degrees Fahrenheit (22 degrees Celsius).

It would also conserve heat from the sun's rays by preventing its loss to outer space. Thus a larger percentage of the sun's radiant energy would be absorbed, uniformly distributed, and retained, than at present.

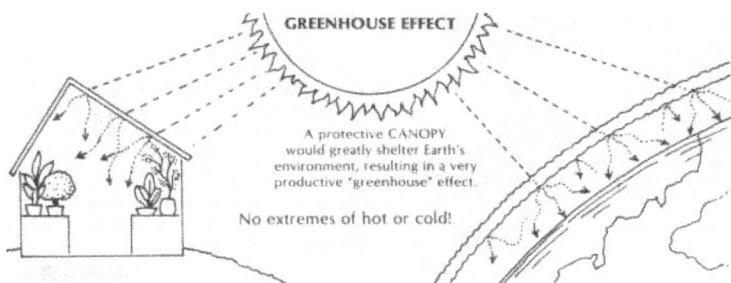

GREENHOUSE EFFECT

A protective CANOPY would greatly shelter Earth's environment, resulting in a very productive "greenhouse" effect.

No extremes of hot or cold!

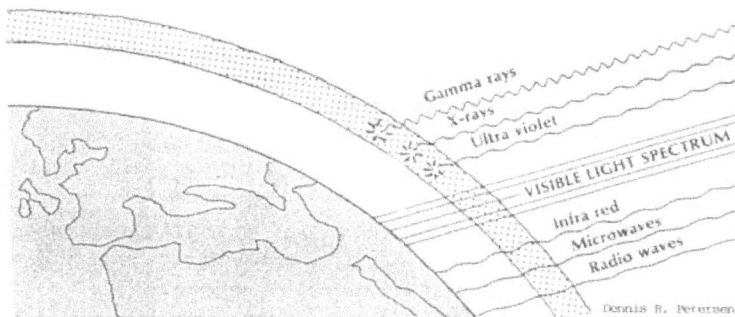

Gamma rays
X-rays
Ultra violet
VISIBLE LIGHT SPECTRUM
Infra red
Microwaves
Radio waves

Dennis R. Petersen

This canopy was probably invisible to earth's inhabitants. It also formed a huge orbital lense, causing the stars to appear larger and much more numerous than they would appear to people on earth today. Of which we shall speak later.

The probability of a water blanket around the earth in the past is put forward seriously by competent men of science. Dr. A.E. Ringwood concluded as much in a paper submitted to the Lunar Science Conference at Houston, Texas, in January, 1970. He stated that early in the earth's history it had a massive atmosphere, at a high enough temperature to evaporate certain elements collected by the earth as it moved through space. [2]

33

The possibility of a massive atmospheric envelope can be taken seriously.

As the water was in orbit and could not be reached by the nuclei of condensation that are needed for cloud formation, rain was unknown until the Great Flood.

There were no upsets in nature. The earth was, at that time, very different.

Again I've mentioned the Great Flood. There are many modern skeptics who will express doubt that such an event ever occurred. And that character, Noah... Well, prepare for a shock or two. In later chapters, we shall uncover some surprising evidence - enough to make your head reel.

But back now to the earth that was. *There were no upsets in nature.* That world was so different from ours.

No wonder the Great Flood was deemed "impossible"! One can understand why that "crackpot" Noah, when he broadcast the message given him that the world would be destroyed by a Flood, was disbelieved. It was a fearful and unheard of thing that God had threatened to bring upon the planet. It was unscientific, unreasonable, and nobody considered it possible. The great masses of the people were against him.

The ancient manuscripts put it this way: "By faith Noah, when warned by God *of things not seen as yet*, moved with holy fear, built a boat to save his family; and by so doing condemned the world." [3]

But we won't go into that. For now, let's take just another look at that water canopy...

EFFECT OF THE CANOPY - SUMMARISED

Let's compare today's world with a CANOPIED environment.

Today, our equatorial zones get the brunt of the sun's heat. Polar regions get little heat. Temperatures on this planet are extreme. As a result of these hot and cold air masses meeting turbulently, today's weather patterns and continual storms are experienced.

But just imagine a controlled terrarium state. Diffused sunlight and heat would result in:

*   a moderate warm climate everywhere

*   no winds and storms

* a continual growing season

* no encroaching wastelands of desert or ice

* lush vegetation worldwide

* protection from harmful cosmic radiation.

Our present limited vapour blanket in our atmosphere is the very thing that makes life possible on earth today.

Originally, a vast canopy of water above the earth's atmosphere must have extended far out into space as a great protective blanket for the beautiful earth.

This virtual wall of water filtered or reflected most of the cosmic and short-wave length radiations that now reach the earth.

What could the results be? These two instantly come to mind:

1. Possible longer life spans
2. Possible larger specimens of some plants and animals.

Is there any evidence suggesting this was so?

Let's find out…

4

The first world (c) -

LOBSTER AS BIG AS A MAN

As I write this, I am in shock.

Believe me, my head is spinning. I'm sitting in my lounge room trying to take it in. If this thing is real… and it is… Well, let me start with the news.

"Bones of an alligator which was as long as a house and as tall as its ceilings have been found on the banks of the Amazon River in South America. Scientists estimate from the alligator's 1.5 metre skull that it was about 2.5 metres [8 feet] tall, and about 12 metres [40 feet] long. Professor Carl Frailey, from Overland Park, Kansas, said the creature probably weighed around 12 tonnes.

" 'This would make it about a tonne heavier than Tyrannosaurus rex… the mightiest of dinosaur predators', he said.

"A spokesman from the *Guinness Book of Records* said this alligator would have been the largest predator yet known. It would appear in the next edition as such."

This news report appeared in *The Sunday Mail* (Brisbane, Australia) on November 17, 1991, on page 3.

Just try to imagine it, will you? Are you sitting in a room with an eight-foot ceiling? Now, fill up the whole room with its head and go from there, right back through the house. That's all alligator.

This chapter is about giants. And in a later chapter we shall talk about living longer. That's how it used to be.

GIANTS

The ancient world was able to support animal and plant life of fantastic size and numbers.

This is what the fossil remains tell us:

1. There was a wider and more even distribution of plant and animal life.
2. There was a greater variety of plants and animals than now.
3. Organisms were of a greater size and quality.

Yes, there has been a distinct deterioration of today's animals and plants compared with the same organisms in fossil form.

Fossil remains show that all terrestrial life has decreased in size. The largest members of the animal kingdom are either becoming extinct, or shrinking as if touched by a magic wand.

- Animals

Mammals were often twice the size of their current counterparts. Here are some examples:

- kangaroos as large as hippopotamuses, with skulls 3 feet long

Size comparison

- horses with 13 inch (32 cm) hoof marks
- koalas as big as rhinos
- elephants with tusks 14 feet (4 m) long
- sheep as big as today's horses
- boars as large as hippopotamuses
- baboons 13 feet (4 metres) tall
- rhinos about 17 feet high and nearly 30 feet long

And the list continues...

- In the northwest of South Australia, between 500 and 1,000 skeletons were found of a colossal wombat as large as a rhinoceros! It was given the name Diprotodon.
- In the Himalayas, tortoises were found with carapices 20 feet long.
- Zoologists from Christchurch, New Zealand, chipped out of a cave roof a fossil skeleton of a penguin 7 feet tall.
- There are fossil eagles 40 feet long and 12 feet high.
  Getting down to smaller creatures:
- We find dragonflies 18 inches long with wings up to 30 inches (75 cm) across - modern wingspan is only about 4 inches (10 cm).
- Some cockroaches were as much as a foot long (30 cm). Can you imagine that? (But no problem, because the hyper-oxygenisation of the aqueous medium – water – would have totally removed the threat of anaerobicic bacteria. I shall explain this hyper-oxygenisation of the original world in the very next chapter.)
- And 6 to 10 feet frogs (2 to 3 metres), had 20 inch heads (50 cm), and jaws more powerful than those of a modern ox.
- Imagine lobsters 6 feet (2 metres) long! They really were.
- And bats the size of sheep, with wingspreads of 15 feet (5 metres).
- Locusts with a 7 inch wingspread
- And scorpions 9 feet long
- Snails almost a foot across

Pre-Flood lobster

Modern man

38

This is not fantasy; their remains are found today, buried in the rubble of the old world.

JUST IMAGINE
AN ALLIGATOR
AS BIG AS A
HOUSE !!!

- Coiled shellfish today grow to about 8 inches across, but fossilised specimens displayed in museums measure over 60 inches.

- Plants
Plant life likewise was gigantic:
- Mosses grew 2 or 3 feet in height, instead of just an inch or so, as they do today.
- Horsetail reeds today usually grow to 5 or 6 feet in height. They used to be up to 50 feet tall.
- I recall reading somewhere of fossil trees that were up to a thousand feet tall (300 metres)!
Yes, it was such a different world.

Amongst the fossils, *giant forms* have been discovered *of almost every kind of creature alive today.*

- Dinosaurs
This discussion would be incomplete if we failed to mention those famous giants called dinosaurs.

- The gigantosaurus (fossil *lizard*) had a head and neck 40 feet long - and an 80 foot tail. Today's Australian spine-covered lizard (and descendant of the scaly dragons) is only 8 inches.
- In 1986, remains were found in New Mexico of a dinosaur that when alive had been 97 to 120 feet (37 metres) long. This "earth shaker" weighed 60 to 100 tons. (Compare that with the modern bull elephant which weighs 7 tons.)
- The flying pteranodon, 20 feet long, when in the air, would look as big as an elephant in flight.
- The brontosaurus, 60 feet long and 25 feet tall, could drink with ease from the gutter of a two-storied house. (One found in South America was as long as 150 feet - 46 metres!)

A single dinosaur would probably have eaten up to 400 tons of food a day. ONLY A SUPER-FERTILE WORLD COULD HAVE SUPPORTED DINOSAURS IN THE FOSSIL NUMBERS.

- Giant humans

There is a belief that the ancient world had 30 percent oxygen in its atmosphere, against our 20 percent. When oxygen concentration increases it encourages gigantism.

From all over the globe, skeletons, artefacts, fossil footprints, houses and tombs speak of a vanished world of massive men and women, to whom very little must have seemed forbidding; people who, born to an incredible lifespan, pursued from strength to strength almost limitless goals. The superiority, the nobility, of this race, we their descendants have all but forgotten.

For some time after the Great Disaster, gigantism continued to a limited extent.

Well-known zoologist Ivan T. Sanderson, who was also a frequent guest on Johnny Carson's *Tonight Show* in the 1960s, received a letter from an engineer who was stationed on Shemya Island in the Aleutians during World War II. While bulldozing for a new airstrip, his crew discovered under several layers of sediment what appeared to be human remains. The mound was actually a graveyard of gigantic human remains.

Fascinating discoveries such as this have been made all over the world. The evidence of giant humans, animals and plants in the past is so widespread that it has motivated me to publish a book on the subject. It is called *The Lost World of Giants*.

Says English scientist Alfred Russell Wallace: "It is quite clear, therefore, that we live in a zoologically impoverished world, from which all the hugest and fiercest and strangest forms have disappeared." [1]

Darwin was astonished to discover that "now we find mere pigmies compared with the antecedent allied races." [2]

Darwin, though hesitating to accept that the situation was changed by a great world catastrophe, could offer no satisfactory solution.

THE SIGNIFICANCE OF THIS

Basic to the theory of evolution is the idea that as an animal evolves to a more complex form, it also increases in size. The very existence of these giant fossils is therefore an embarrassment to the evolution theory. These discoveries are usually ignored by evolutionists as far as possible.

The simple truth is, essentially everything in the fossil record is larger than its modern counterpart.

The gigantism that has been unearthed turns out to be predicted by the neglected biblical account.

So when the denigrated book of Genesis tells us "there were giants in the earth in those days", [3] it is evidently recording not myth, but FACT.

IF YOU DO NOT BELIEVE THAT IT IS POSSIBLE FOR MAN TO DECREASE IN STATURE AS ILLUSTRATED HERE, THEN HOW IS IT THAT **PYGMIES** AND **DWARFS** ??

15 FEET

6 FEET

ADAM NOAH MODERN-DAY MAN & WOMAN!

Sketch: Jim Pinkoski

Giant human footprints in Cretaceous strata, Paluxy Rver, Texas

5

The first world (d) -

IF A SNAKE BITES YOU...

"Can you believe it? My tomato plant is as high as a 3-story building!"

"Yes... yes..." Kei's neighbour suppressed a smirk as he politely heard out the mad scientist. Too much learning, poor chap. It had pushed him over the brink. It was time his family had him put away in a safe place.

Here's an amazing story of giant tomatoes from a plant that just kept on living. Let me tell you what happened.

Japanese physicist Dr. Kei Mori of Kao University in Tokyo exposed plant life to two of the conditions of the original world ecology. He grew tomato plants under a plastic dome which filtered the ultraviolet rays; and he increased the carbon-dioxide.

After two years, a cherry tomato plant was 16 feet tall, with 903 tomatoes on it. After six years, the same tomato plant was over 30 feet tall and had produced over 5,000 tomatoes.

That tomato plant just didn't want to die. Ask yourself now, How long do tomato plants usually live? Perhaps five or six months? They die of old age, destroyed by ultra-violet radiation.

Could this have some bearing on how old people would have lived under the same environment?

ATMOSPHERIC PRESSURE

The atmospheric pressure, as well as the oxygen content, had to be greater in the past, in order to support the huge life forms which then existed.

Dr. Carl Baugh, of Glen Rose Texas, has set out to build the world's first hyperbaric biosphere, 62 feet long. Its purpose is to simulate the context of our original world. An engineer from NASA has called it the greatest experiment ever performed in the name of science, in history.

Among a selection of small creatures placed into an experimental prototype of this first ever biosphere were two snakes.

It was decided to test the snake venom. Over a period of time, Carl had the snakes milked three times.

In the first test (before the snakes were placed in the biosphere) their venom looked like a lump of spaghetti – all together. After a period inside the biosphere, the snakes were milked again. And their venom still looked like spaghetti – but now the lump was separated. After a longer time in the biosphere, they were again milked and their venom examined. It now looked like honeycomb.

Disorder had been transformed into order.

Snake venom viewed with a scanning electron microscope is gnarled and unstructured. The sulphide bonds in snake venom produce the toxic agent under such conditions.

But when ultra violet light is eliminated and the atmosphere pressure is doubled (simulating conditions that existed in the original world) the venom regains its structure.

Dr. Baugh believes that in the atmosphere of the original world, a snake bite would give an injection of protein, rather than poison. And possibly such pests as mosquitoes might not have resorted to attacking humans, since they were satisfied on the nutrients in plants.

Says Dr. Baugh:

"We've been doing extensive research into the ancient atmosphere, the one that produced the fossil record. Our research indicates that essentially everything was larger in the past. For instance, the club mosses which today reach sixteen to eighteen inches often approach two hundred feet in the fossil record. The great dinosaurs, with their relatively small lung capacity, reached tremendous stature. Seismosaurus could reach his head almost seventy feet in the air. Something has to explain this anomaly in terms of today's atmosphere."

The difference may well be in the atmospheric pressure:

"In today's atmosphere we have 14.7 pounds atmospheric pressure per inch at sea level. But to oxygenate the deep cell tissue of these great dinosaurs we need much greater atmospheric pressure. Research has shown that when you approach two times today's atmospheric pressure, the entire blood plasma is saturated with oxygen….

"Our research indicates there was about 27 pounds per square inch of atmospheric pressure [in the past]. That would beautifully solve a problem even paleontologists admit exists.

"In addition, the oxygen supply in the fossil record has been found to be 30 percent oxygen compared to 20 percent today. Ancient air bubbles trapped in amber have been analysed and revealed this heavier concentration of oxygen. If we had those conditions today, we could run two hundred miles without fatigue." [1]

In summary, the atmosphere possessed more carbon-dioxide and oxygen (one of the by-products of vigorous plant growth).

ATMOSPHERIC PRESSURE
PROMOTED RAPID HEALING

Some time ago, a man inside a bathyscope deep under the sea had a nasty accident, in which his hand was badly gashed. However, it was a clean cut, so he pressed the wound shut and wrapped it around with a cloth.

The surface crew wanted to bring him back up immediately for treatment, but this was not possible, due to the fact that the bathyscope was pressurised within, to compensate for the heavy outside water pressure at that depth. Gradual decompression would take several hours.

So it was decided that the diver should stay down until morning.

When he resurfaced, and the bandage was removed, what was their surprise to discover the wound well on the way to being healed!

It seems that the pre-Flood atmosphere, in the event of an injury, served to promote faster healing.

Something else. The atmospheric pressure, as well as the oxygen content, would have had to be greater in the past, in order to support the huge life forms which then existed. This would have required some kind of canopy above the earth. To provide such a quantity of oxygen as required by the larger life forms, the oxygen would need to approach the level of toxicity, unless the atmospheric pressure was greater.

In West Texas, a fossilised flying reptile, known as a pterodactyl, has been found, with a wingspan of 52 feet.

There is no way such a "flying dinosaur" could have flown with today's atmospheric pressure. However, with atmospheric pressure of around 32 pounds per square inch, it would have been a piece of cake.

CANOPY WOULD PROMOTE
SUCH ATMOSPHERIC PRESSURE

Now envision the water canopy around the earth. Think of the effect this would have upon the atmospheric pressure.

A document thousands of years old, in describing the pre-Flood earth, speaks of a "firmament" above the earth, encased by layers of water above and below it. [2]

Baugh calls this ancient canopy "this double bubble of crystalline water".

He notes that approximately eleven miles above the surface of our earth there exists a heat sink.

"It is between −130 degrees Fahrenheit and −180 degrees Fahrenheit at that elevation. Nearer to the earth it is warmer, and further from the earth it is warmer for at least some space. If we were to amass the amounts of water present on Earth, and assimilate the greater amount of water within the earth, this would leave the approximate remainder of a ten-to-twenty-feet thick lineal dimension double encasement of water in solid crystalline form as the firmament." [3]

According to Dr. Baugh this "firmament" was "apparently in crystalline form – pure, transparent, relatively thin ice. It was probably no more than twenty feet thick at best… The word used in the Hebrew to describe the firmament is *raqiya*. Hebrew scholars recognise that the word *raqiya* means to compress or pound out, and stretch out this arch of heaven in thin metal sheets." [4]

This "firmament" apparently consisted of a layer of water, or compressed hydrogen, which extended completely around the earth.

Indeed, the possibility of a massive atmospheric envelope can be taken seriously.

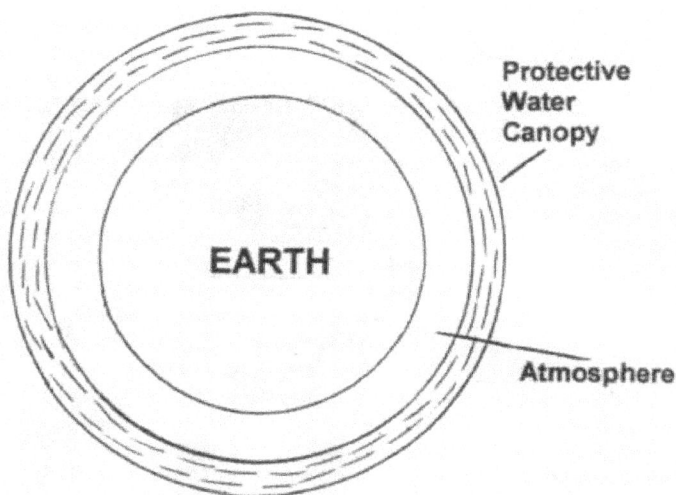

Protective Water Canopy

EARTH

Atmosphere

EFFECT OF A CANOPY
ON THE ATMOSPHERE

With such a canopy, the atmosphere would be pressurised to a greater degree than we have now.

"Researchers, like Dr. Henry Voss, at the University of Illinois, have been able to approximate the atomic weight of such a canopy. This crystalline canopy would put a cap on the atmosphere. Atmospheric pressure today at sea level is 14.7 pounds per square inch." [5] The air pressure of the world before the Great Disaster would have been about two times what it is today.

Do we have evidence of this? Indeed, we do.

SURPRISING EVIDENCE
– A PRE-FLOOD HAMMER

In June, 1934, near London, Texas, members of the Hahn family discovered by a waterfall on Red Creek a rock with wood protruding from it. They chiselled it open, exposing a hammer head. The petrified hammer was found in a layer of Cretaceous sandstone. The handle was fossilised with a blackened coal tip.

Scientists opposed to the idea that man-made objects could be found in rock "more than 100 million years old" associated with dinosaurs have expressed skepticism since the artefact was not found in situ by professionals.

Photo © 1992 by David Lines

However, in the 1980s, Dr. Baugh took this artefact to the Batelle Laboratories in Columbus, Ohio, the same laboratory that analysed moonstones. The elemental analysis showed it to be 96.6 percent iron, 0.74 percent sulphur, and 2.6 percent chlorine.

Physicists tell us that under today's atmospheric conditions you cannot compound chlorine with metallic iron. Yet here it is. Today, chlorine can be joined with iron as solid metal *only in two atmospheres of oxygen pressure*, and *only in the absence of ultraviolet radiation.*

Of course, ultraviolet radiation would have been filtered out by the protective canopy.

Research indications are that the pre-Flood atmosphere is the only plausible explanation, for the forging of this metallic artefact.

There is evidence that the oxygen ratio of the atmosphere was then 30 percent, compared with 21 percent today; and that the carbon-dioxide ratio was 2 percent, as against 0.035 percent today.

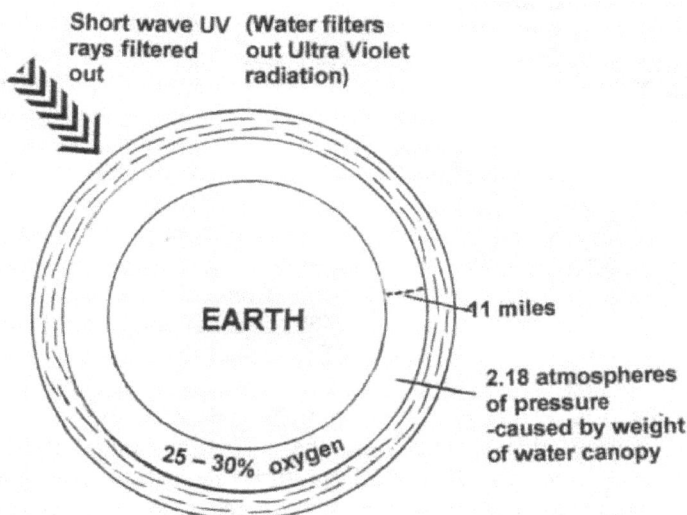

Short wave UV rays filtered out (Water filters out Ultra Violet radiation)

EARTH

11 miles

2.18 atmospheres of pressure -caused by weight of water canopy

25 – 30% oxygen

Note: Dr Mori raised plants under special light that filtered out IR and UV radiation. His unique process of fiberoptic sunlight collection and transmission, called "Himawari Sunlighting" is now marketed worldwide. After extensive experiments Mori claimed the filtered light, far from being detrimental, could actually promote healing. His conclusion was that "because the ultraviolet is blocked, this sunlight does not fade fabrics or damage skin." [6] One long-lived tomato plant was grown in a special nutrient-rich solution to be exhibited at the Japan Expo '85. Under piped sunlight and controlled atmosphere, this tomato tree grew over 30 ft high and yielded more than 13,000 ripe tomatoes during the six months of the Expo! [7]

6

The first world (e) -

ANCIENT NUCLEAR REACTOR

Did you know that most metals in their purer state are TRANSPARENT?

When our astronauts went to the moon, they wore visors coated with transparent gold – and they could see through them clearly. The gold protected them – shielded them – from cosmic radiation.

(That reminds me that a 2,000 year old book – the "Revelation" – speaks of transparent gold. [1]

METALLIC WATER

During their research on the hydrogen bomb, physicists at Laurence Livermore National laboratories took the elements of water and compressed them under super-cold, cryogenic temperatures. Hydrogen (an element of water) became near-metallic in form. It took on the characteristics of metal. It became transparent, fibre-optic, superconductive, ferromagnetic and crystalline.

The implications of this are tremendous, if we consult a very ancient description of our planet as it once used to be.

The Hebrew book of Genesis is not a book on science, yet investigation into some of its statements, on occasions when it dips into scientific matters, has astonished me with its scientific accuracy. In its unique way, Genesis states that above our earth the Creator stretched a "firmament". This "firmament" was in the middle, with water above and water beneath.

The Hebrew word for "firmament", as we noted earlier, is *raqiya*, which means to press, or pound together into thin metal sheets. This seems to imply that the canopy, or arch of the heavens, was formed and stretched out around this earth in thin metal sheets.

One may be puzzled by this metallic description of the "firmament" given in Genesis. However, as an archaeologist working on other projects in the Middle East, I have learned that it pays to take ancient biblical statements literally, just as the writer intended. And in doing so, it has been possible to solve questions that still elude some other archaeologists.

It was that same approach to Homer that enabled Schliemann to discover Troy.

So what is Genesis trying to tell us? Why is this metallic description of the "firmament" given in Genesis?

It is now known that under super-cold conditions, with great pressure and tremendous energy, the hydrogen in water binds together in a crystalline lattice.

One can envision a canopy above the earth consisting of compressed energized hydrogen taking on near-metallic characteristics. This would be in the middle of a solid water formation suspended about eleven miles above the earth.

According to the laws of physics, this canopy, to avoid being absorbed into the atmosphere, would have needed to be a solid canopy.

NOT TOTALLY DARK AT NIGHT

Such a canopy, being crystalline and ferromagnetic, would transfer energy.

The energy of the sun upon this layer of hydrogen would cause a gentle pink glow. This is the colour that is produced by energized hydrogen.

During the day, the greater penetration of light would produce varying shades of pink. The lowest pink hue would be at noon, due to the angle of the light passing through the firmament canopy.

In the lesser light of night a deeper shade of pink was seen, in addition to an enhanced moon. At sunrise and sunset it was a vivid pink; and at midnight the sky appeared magenta pink.

When it was night on one side of the planet, there would be a transfer of energy from the day side of the earth along the curved lines of the canopy. Electro-magnetic energy would be carried along the lines of near-metallic hydrogen, which was fibre-optic in nature.

The result would be a twilight glow on the night side of the earth - a "lesser light" ruling the night. Earth's inhabitants never saw total darkness.

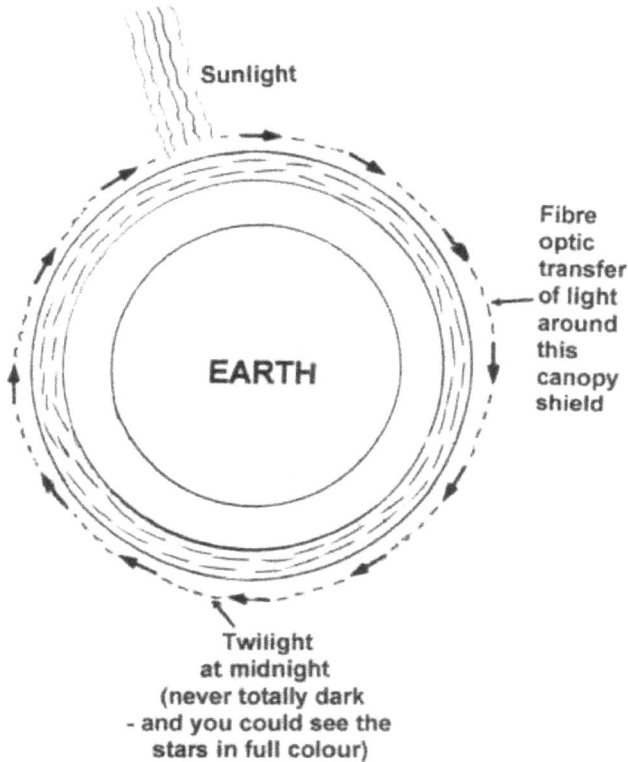

Sunlight

Fibre optic transfer of light around this canopy shield

EARTH

Twilight
at midnight
(never totally dark
- and you could see the
stars in full colour)

EFFECT OF THE PINK GLOW

Scientists and researchers are discovering that the most important colour in the entire spectrum is pink. Energized hydrogen in the canopy giving off the pink glow helped to contribute to the enormous size of plant life.

Biologists have found that under pink light the greatest plant growth is encouraged. It is pink light which optimally triggers the growth of cells within plants. Not only do plants grow better under pink light, but people respond in mood to pink light. Under the right spectrum of pink light, the brain secretes norepinephren, which is a natural tranquilliser and neurotransmitter.

In the antedeluvian (pre-Flood) world, the various spectra of pink light dominated, with a gentle pink glow day and night. The tranquillity of man's environment contributed to his brain working at maximum efficiency.

STARS MAGNIFIED

The invisible canopy formed a huge orbital lense, causing the stars to appear larger and much more numerous than they would appear to people on earth today. In those days the stars would appear about three times brighter. They would have been magnified and photomultiplied with vibrant colour.

Ancient records among many cultures recall a time in the past when the sky "hung low" – appearing closer.

As a matter of fact, I was this morning reminded of this when I read the report of an Australian Aboriginal legend. It speaks of a time when "the sky was close to the ground" and of an event in which "Yondi raised the sky". [2]

This myth conveys the startling difference between the antedeluvian heavens and the sky as it is viewed in the present age.

NASA discovered some years ago that not only are stars emitting radio wave energy, but that there is a music on those radio waves. And to their amazement they found that the music being emitted is in a major key – it is harmonious.

Astonished scientists compared the music being emitted from these star sources to the instruments of an orchestra that are all in tune with each other. [3]

Imagine it! Radio waves passing through the canopy and radiating sound - a beautiful harmony of sound!

The stars, as we know, shine in various colours – some are red, others gold, or green, yellow, amber, and so on.

In that original world, a person looking up through the canopy could see the stars in beautiful full colour.

Each morning, as the earth rotated toward the sun, when the angle was just right, the radio waves from the universe would be amplified by the crystalline canopy. (You may be aware that crystals amplify long radio waves.) Thus this "music" could be heard on earth.

Whilst the canopy would permit the long waves of energy to go right through it, it would filter out the harmful shortwave radiation. What a wonderful world! It's as though all this was intentionally put together!

HOW THE EARTH WAS HEATED

Today our atmosphere is heated primarily by shortwave energy from outer space.

However, in the original world this would not have been so. The shortwave energy was filtered out by the firmament canopy. The heating of the environment was not from above, but from a gentle thermal blanket within the earth itself.

Radio-active elements now in sedimentary rocks on the surface of our planet were once *inside* the earth. In the Great Disaster, these isotopes were expunged, or thrown out, to the earth's surface.

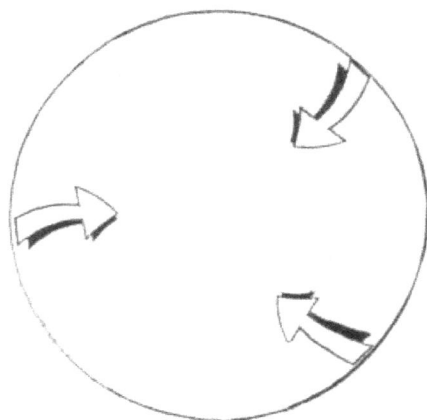

RADIO-ACTIVE ELEMENTS now in sedimentary rocks (since the Flood) -were once INSIDE the earth (before the Flood)

The heat inside our planet cannot be explained satisfactorily by pressure and reaction. It can be explained only by nuclear reaction.

Originally, the earth's interior contained radioactive material, evenly balanced. Inside the earth, the radio-isotopes (uranium, strontium, rubidium, iridium and radio isotopic lead) were in perfect balance with moderators (such as manganese, sulphur, water and magnesium) adjacent to them.

Thus the interior of the earth was a controlled nuclear reactor.

This would have gently warmed the ground and the atmosphere. At night the temperature would have been about 72 degrees Fahrenheit (22 Celsius). And about 78 degrees Fahrenheit (25 Celsius) during the day. It's as though the interior of the earth had been deliberately designed for the benefit of mankind.

DESIGNED TO LAST FOREVER

The fissionable material inside the earth was designed to go forever, even as was the human body designed to be renewable. There existed what physicists would term a breeder reactor. As long as there was a constant energy input into the system, there would always be as many elements as you started with.

A continuous input of energy from stellar space was absorbed into the crystalline canopy. The electromagnetic field of the canopy transferred this energy to the electromagnetic of the di-pole magnet of the earth. In this manner the energy supply was constantly restructured and replaced.

HOW THIS BENEFITED MANKIND

So it was that in the earth's interior we had a perfectly balanced *thermonuclear reactor.*

Above that stretched a *solid crust of granite* around the earth. This crust was (and still is) from six to sixteen miles thick, with massive reservoirs of water retained underneath.

Above the granite crust there would have existed a *layer of sand or silicon*, the element that is the most common worldwide.

And vegetation would have been above this silicon layer. In the total context, there would have been a warming of the root systems, for superior growth. Experiments show that when plant roots are warmed just 2 to 5 degrees Fahrenheit, they produce 30 to 50 percent more foliage and fruit.

And growing under pink light, with the amount of carbon dioxide slightly increased, and shielded from ultraviolet rays, the plants would grow better still. Add to that an increased atmospheric pressure permitting the absorption of more oxygen, and plant life could grow to abundance and to enormous proportions. There would be a continual growing season.

This would also dictate the size of certain forms of animal life. Certainly, these were optimal circumstances in which to live.

Just imagine superior man with a perfect environment, perfect foods with complete nutrition… and no life threatening cosmic radiation.

A PARADISE WORLD

Add to that the lush scenery. In visible beauty, the world was "perfect". Today's most enchanting islands in the South seas are a mere echo of that forgotten world.

Its landscape was refreshingly varied, from dry ridge to marshy expanse, from warm tropical valley to mild mountaintop. It was decked with surface mineral riches and lavished with bounties. The gaining of a livelihood must have been easy.

It is not mere speculation to describe that first world as a real paradise, because its mummified remains, found in abundance all over the world, do not lie. Just as Egypt's pyramids and the ancient monuments are evidence of once great civilizations, so do the fossils speak eloquently of the glories of a world which has passed away.

It looks like we had a wonder world… and somebody blew it.

7

The first world (f) -

COULD YOU REALLY LIVE TO BE 600?

"He's too old. It's time to kill him!" Old Olaf cringed as he overhead his family planning his demise. But he couldn't escape. That was the custom on these Hebrides Islands, off the coast of Scotland.

There have been some big changes over the years. And one of these is how long we live.

So how long do you think we could live, given the chance?

And that brings me to another question: *WAS THERE A TIME WHEN LONG LIFE WAS REALLY WITHIN OUR GRASP?*

The answer to the second question is… YES. THERE WAS THAT TIME.

RACIAL TRADITIONS

Everything in the "pre-Flood" environment favoured the continued production of larger, stronger, longer-lived specimens of every type of creature. The fossil record confirms this picture.

It should be noted that the memory of past long life in mankind is found in nearly all traditional writings. The best known, of course, is the Bible. It states very plainly that early man enjoyed a life expectancy of almost a thousand years.

It is difficult to conceive of anything like this today; it is much easier to be skeptical.

Nevertheless, accounts of man once living to a great age occur in the folklores and traditions of almost every ancient race. Egypt, Syria, Persia, India and Greece all possess traditions of a long-lived race during a previous age.

- Theopompus (c.378-300 B.C.) stated that a now sunken land was inhabited by men of gigantic size who lived twice as long as now.

- A Transylvanian gipsy tradition relates that "there was a time when men lived forever and when neither worry nor sickness troubled them. Meat and fruits existed in abundance, and the rivers flowed with milk and wine. Men and animals lived happy lives and were without fear of death." Then came a worldwide Flood. [1]
- Flavius Josephus, Jewish historian, cited earlier historians who claimed "that the ancients lived a thousand years." [2]
- The Chibchas of Peru have a legend of a hero who lived for 2,000 years.
- The people of Yunnan, China, have preserved the memory of an age when all were prosperous and lived hundreds of years.
- The Greeks and Romans suggested ages of 800 to 1,000 years (reminding us of the biblical figures).

If we are to believe that such records are based on a core of truth, then something dramatic must have happened. What changed the situation?

Since this change occurred, the average life span of mankind has remained relatively constant over the past 3,000 years, though on rare occasions, certain individuals may live considerably longer.

- In eastern India, even in historical times, there were people who lived 400 years, according to Pliny and Solinus.
- In the Hebrides Islands, west of Scotland, there existed the custom of putting to death those who, after 150 to 200 years, had become so decrepit, that they were considered useless.
- In 1933, the *New York Times* announced the death of Professor Li Chung Yun who, born in 1677, had attained his 256th birthday. Those who saw him claimed he did not appear older than 52! He had outlived 23 wives and was living with his 24th at the time.
- In 1956, Mrs Maria Garson Viuda de Castaneda of Cucunuba produced a birth certificate in Bogota, Columbia, showing she was born December 30, 1778. Medical evidence supported her claim to be 177.
- As recently as 2003, the *Guardian* newspaper (United Kingdom) announced that a woman at least 124 years old

had been found in the war-torn republic of Chechnya. Zabani Khachukayeva's passport stated that she is 124 years old. Doctors, however, believed she may be even older. Apart from having impaired hearing, she was declared to be in relatively good health and said that she still felt energetic.

Khachukayeva had outlived her eldest son, who died in 2001, and enjoyed 24 grandchildren, 38 great-grandchildren, and 7 great-great-grandchildren.

Warren Matthews commented: "There you go. It is possible to live to 120 years of age free from disease and still retain all of your faculties! Ever wondered how these people who live a long time in good health usually come from poor parts of the world and do not have the benefit of the so called 'health' system that we have in the Western world? Maybe they can thank the lack of exposure to modern pharmaceutical drugs for their long life? What do you think?"

Western scientists question such claims, including those found in the Bible. Judgment is made on present day experience and birth records of this century - the oldest age on record verified with certainty being around 120 years. Yet 17th- to 19th century historical records discussed in textbooks on gerontology (the study of old age) are replete with ages of up to 188 years, in Europe.

- The oldest living person in 1973 was claimed to be Shirali Mislimov. He was living at Barzavu in Azerbaijan on the Iranian border. His age was alleged to be 167.

Nevertheless, American scientists refused to believe it. One can only assess local records and testimonies. There is no other way to measure a person's absolute age.

- I recall a news report of another man in that general region who was said to be 165 years old. He had not spoken to his son for 20 years, because the naughty young 143 year old had married a woman of whom his father did not approve!

BUT IF SCIENTISTS CAN'T BELIEVE PEOPLE WHO ARE STILL LIVING TODAY, HOW WILL THEY EVER BELIEVE PEOPLE WHO LIVED THOUSANDS OF YEARS AGO?

PERHAPS WE SHOULD BE SKEPTICAL EVEN OF OUR SKEPTICISM?

Until recent years, such figures might well be regarded as absurd. However, today's medical standards and investigations of this question have reached a point where such claims can no longer be totally ignored, nor denied with a certainty that permits no doubt of any kind.

For the moment, it can be said confidently that there is historical evidence to support the Bible's account and no scientific reasons for doubting it.

The fact that we do not now live for 800 to 900 years does not mean that such longevity was never possible.

WHAT SOME SCIENTISTS SAY

There are scientists who readily accept longer life as a reality.

In fact, there is no biological reason why human beings die at the comparatively early age of 60 to 70 years. SEPARATED CELL TISSUES HAVE BEEN KEPT ALIVE UNDER SUITABLE CONDITIONS FOR AN INDEFINITE PERIOD.

U.S. scientist Dr. Patrick Flanagan reported to author Alan Landsburg:

"We've had cells taken from the human body live in a nutrient solution inside a pyramid shape *NINE TIMES* THEIR NORMAL LIFE SPAN." [3]

Experiments on human fibroblasts conducted by Dr. Hayflick showed fifty population doublings to be the limit of cellular life. When other experimenters added Vitamin E to the nutrient solution, the life span of the cultures was more than doubled. [4]

Professor Gennady Bardyshev, writing in the newspaper *Sovietskaya Rossiya*, foresees the possibility of man living for 200 years. He said experiments showed that by adding flat-fish fats to animal fodder, it was possible to increase animals' life span by 15 to 20 percent.

Dr Linus C. Pauling, world-renowned chemist, winner of two Nobel prizes and one of the most original thinkers of our time, states:

"Death is unnatural…. Theoretically, man is quite immortal. His body tissues replace themselves. He is a self-repairing machine.

And yet he gets old and dies, and the reasons for this are still a mystery." [5]

Dr. Alex Comfort, director of research in gerontology at University College, London, adds his opinion:

"If we kept throughout life the same resistance to stress, injury and disease that we had at the age of ten, about one half of us here today might expect to survive in 700 years' time." [6]

"LIVE TO BE 1,000," says a Cambridge scientist in an article in *BBC News Online*, 3 Dec 2004.

Geneticist Aubrey de Grey claims a project named Strategies for Engineered Negligible Senescence will be able to "repair all the types of molecular and cellular damage that happen to us over time."

De Grey is confident of his claim because some of the repair methods needed have already been developed and are undergoing clinical trials, and others are based on technologies that already exist but need to be applied to the problem of ageing. Parts of the project should be working in mice within 10 years and it may only take another 10 to be working in humans. On the basis of these developments, de Grey thinks the first person to live to be 1,000 may already be 60.

Says Dr. Hans Selys, Director of the Institute of Experimental Surgery of Montreal University:

"Medicine has assembled a fund of knowledge that will now serve, I believe, as a point of departure for studying the causes of old age. If the causes of ageing can be found, there is no good medical reason to believe that it will not be possible for science to find some practical way of slowing the process down, or even bringing it to a standstill." [7]

"Someday we may live almost indefinitely." So said Dr. Bernard Strehler, a biologist at the University of Southern California, according to *Newsweek*.

So much for what some scientists have been saying.

WHEN DID WE LOSE IT?

According to the ancient records, something extremely significant happened to the earth and to man at the time of the Great Flood. Whatever it was, it probably removed the dominant factor for long life.

Still, you may want to ask at this point, can we really place much credence in ancient legends?

Surprisingly, a great deal. Too often, I'm afraid, we have been prone to dismiss folklore and mythology out of hand. But is this not unscientific, especially since traditions have often led us to discover physical remains?

LEGENDS ARE USUALLY BASED ON A CORE OF FACT

Pertinently, William Prescott, the great Americanologist, reminds us: "A nation may pass away and leave only the memory of its existence, but the stories of science it has gathered up will endure forever." [8]

You see, folklore is a fossil of history. It preserves history in the guise of colourful tales. Far from being a collection of fables, it is a recital of actual past events, even though from generation to generation some facts have become distorted or forgotten.

We must face it: traditions are usually based on a core of fact.

Take the legend of Troy. No scholar took *The Iliad* or *The Odyssey* of Homer as history. But Schliemann, putting faith in it, discovered the "mythical" city of Troy. *The Iliad* spoke of a cup decorated with doves which Odysseus used. In a shaft Schliemann found that 3,000-year-old cup.

Mexican Indian legends spoke of a sacred well of sacrifice, into which maidens and jewellery were hurled. Historians dismissed this as a mere tale, until the well, at Chichen Itza, was discovered in the nineteenth century.

More than any document, *the Bible* was assailed as a collection of fanciful myths. Yet, to the embarrassment of the critics, archaeological discoveries proved time and again that the fabled cities, mythical giants and impossible events were true and reliable reporting in every detail. Indeed, the Bible can now be regarded as *the most accurate and trustworthy source of history we possess.*

There is strong evidence as to the historical basis of the ancient traditions. We should be careful about discounting anything that is recorded that seems strange to us. The Bible in particular has an uncanny habit of being proved true.

THE LOSS OF LONGEVITY

Notice the graph below.

Plotting the natural life span of ancient men as given in the biblical chronologies yields a statistically significant curve which surely argues strongly for the validity of the biblical records. [9]

In the biblical chronology, the first "dot" of the chart represents the age of Adam. This is followed by each successive generation. A rapid decline in longevity correlates with the cosmic catastrophe that restructured the world in the time of Noah.

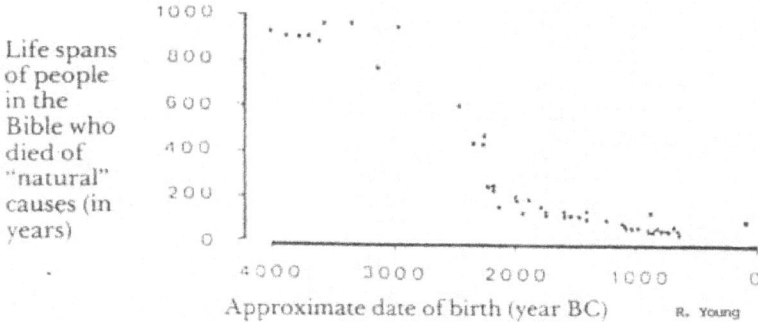

Approximate date of birth (year BC)   R. Young

According to Genesis, the average age was reduced from 857 years before the Flood, to 600 for the Flood survivor Shem, down to 147 by the time of Jacob, about 1850 B.C. By Solomon's time it was 95 years, then down to the Middle Ages, 35 years; and now today, up to 74 years.

Interestingly, the ancient traditions (biblical and non-biblical) all point to a long life span of individuals before the Great Flood, with a gradual decrease of life span afterward, until we reach the well-known three-score and ten of historical times.

For example, the long ages recorded in the Sumerian King List are suddenly reduced after the Flood to about 100 years. This compares to a similar rapid decrease in the biblical record.

And scientific findings agree. Studies of so-called cave men from various European sites (for example those of the Cro-Magnon group) likewise indicate an early death for many.

A combination of factors seem to determine this result: a harsher environment after the Flood, poor diet and lack of sunshine in more northerly latitudes in particular (with consequent proneness to rickets), proliferation of disease, plus a greater propensity for mutations.

WHY LONG LIFE SPANS WERE POSSIBLE

Today the probability of survival over a century is less than one percent.

I can think of several factors which favoured longevity in the past, and others which intervened to bring it to an end.

1.   More vitality

Firstly, the antedeluvian (pre-Flood) race was, according to the ancient records, nearer to original perfection. Man was physically healthier, endowed with considerably *more vitality* than today.

There would have been a richer gene pool in contrast to the depleted pool which prevails today. Also, if the human constitution allowed for a much extended capability of cell multiplication, the body would have greater ability for self-regeneration. These factors could well have contributed not only to a much slower ageing process, but also to an extended procreative capacity.

2.   Rich virgin soil

Antedeluvian man was nourished from *rich virgin soil.* This was devastated by the Great Flood. It washed through the original fertile soils and redeposited them unevenly as regards trace elements.

The seething waters of the Deluge churned up the top soil of the earth's crust. Later, as the waters receded into the newly-opened basins we now call oceans, they tore the fertile soil layer from the surface and flushed it down to the ocean floor, leaving behind a mere vestige of the original nutrients. The remaining water-washed soil lost its primeval fine balance of raw materials, so that plants were unable to supply optimum nutrition, as before.

Even apparently healthy plants in today's soils, while serving as good food sources, may be lacking in some essential element. Lack of iodine in some soils is one example.

In a single cubic mile of sea water there are about 170 million tons of dissolved mineral salts. We do not know how much was originally in the seas, but undoubtedly a large amount has been flushed from the soil.

Thus one factor contributing to our loss of longevity since the Deluge may be the impoverished nutrition.

Ancient records insist that the original diet of all animals was plant matter. Evidently this was rich enough in all necessary nutrients even for those animals which today we consider carnivorous. It is possible that many plant types did not survive the Flood. Consequently many animals with their short digestive tracts were compelled to adopt a flesh diet in order to obtain the required nutrients in sufficient concentration.

Likewise, man turned to eating animal flesh in order to supply deficiencies in a once adequate diet. This change is recorded in the book of Genesis. [10.] Does the short life span of carnivores when compared to the longer life span of herbivores tell us something? At any rate, man's life span decreased.

Today, so deficient is nutrition, that most people on earth go to bed at night on empty stomachs. The favoured sections of our degenerate race now live on vitamin pills.

3.   The radiation factor

One could mention another factor - *radiation*. It is well known that ultra-violet radiation from the sun is largely responsible for "ageing" human tissue.

Radiation can contribute to biological mutations. Genetic mutations cause deterioration in future generations, thus accounting for decreases in size and viability - and even extinctions of many animals. Then there are the somatic mutations in the body cells which cause deterioration and eventual death of the individual exposed to radiation. Such somatic mutations may thus be directly related to loss of longevity.

The radiation-free environment of the pre-Flood world may have been one more factor which contributed to the long lives of humans and the large sizes of flora and fauna. The protective vapour canopy must certainly have had a modifying effect, shielding life forms from cosmic radiation. It filtered out the short wavelength radiations which most actively accelerate the ageing process.

After the Deluge, with the water shell gone, there began the unobstructed bombardment of life-shortening cosmic rays. The mutation rate was speeded up.

The size and strength of the average creature deteriorated. Many species became extinct. And the length of the life span began to decline. (These trends are still apparent today, although modern medicine and sanitation have, to some extent, masked the general trend as far as man is concerned.)

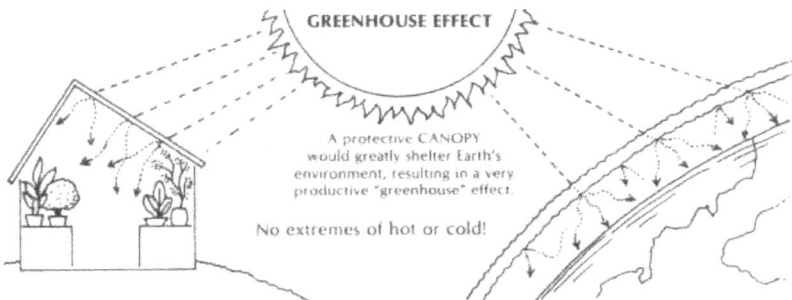

GREENHOUSE EFFECT

A protective CANOPY would greatly shelter Earth's environment, resulting in a very productive "greenhouse" effect.

No extremes of hot or cold!

3.   The climate factor

Another factor could have been the *climate*. As we noticed, the original world enjoyed a more agreeable climate. Stress-producing hurricanes, droughts and floods were unknown.

After the deluge, the healthful subtropical and temperate climates gave way to the frozen ice lands and the unbearably hot tropics of the new planet. Extremes of climate sapped the vital force of man and animals.

5.   Carbon dioxide factor

Before the Deluge, there was, so fossil plant remains suggest, probably more *carbon dioxide* in the air. It is claimed that a "50 percent decrease in the amount of carbon dioxide in the air will lower the average temperature of the earth 6.9 degrees Fahrenheit." [11]

A warmer climate in the past is therefore consistent with a greater concentration of carbon dioxide in the air at that time. Experiments show that with a sharp increase of carbon dioxide, tomatoes will grow and produce much better than in today's normal atmosphere. Such a factor in the pre-Flood world may have been advantageous to life at that time.

6.   The catastrophe factor

According to one theory, *catastrophe itself* could produce genetic mutation. Did the Flood and its traumatic, stressful aftermath (which persisted for centuries) induce a mutation that became the dominant factor in the human gene pool? And did that mutation rob man of his long life span?

7.   Wrong living

Social problems must have emerged from developing a new civilisation in the new, harsh conditions. Linked with this, the effects of *wrong living and disease* must likewise have taken their toll, eventually.

8.   Special intervention

The biblical record suggests yet *another factor: special intervention.* The decree went forth that in view of man's developed capacity for evil, his life span was to be limited. [12] It is the Creator who decides the life span of mankind. Were we, then, programmed to die earlier?

Michael Maconochie reports that one important cause of ageing is "we are probably *programmed to die.* There is almost certainly genetic material in our molecular DNA - the biological building blocks which everyone is made from - which tells the body to switch itself off, permanently, at about 120 years of age."

At universities and medical research centres around the world, the multi-billion dollar Human Genome project is under way. Genetic scientists are attempting a solution to this problem. [13]

QUALITY – NOT JUST LIFE

Meanwhile, would you like to lengthen your life and enjoy it?

Apart from the usual big three - regular exercise, sensible diet and vitamin supplements - Maconochie has this to say:

"Concentrate on grains, vegetables, pulses and fruit - in that order."

Evidently, it does work. The book of Genesis tells us that man's original diet was vegetarian. [14]

Hundreds of studies of one group, the Seventh-day Adventists, have revealed that the lifestyle they follow helps prevent disease, maintain health and promote longevity. Detroit *News* book reviewer Kate De Smet found that half of North American Adventists were strict vegetarians and teetotallers who lived 12 years longer than the general American population and "have lower fatality rates for the 10 leading causes of death in America." [15]

Researcher Chris Rucker added to this his claim that this vegetarian group have more stamina and energy than others and "feel and behave decades younger than their years. They refuse to believe that aches and pains are a normal part of the ageing process, nor do they believe that mental deterioration is inevitable." [16]

In this regard, Maconochie's point is relevant:

"Living forever loses its attraction, however, if we simply age, then live indefinitely in a fragile, disease-prone state. What's the point of being 120 if we can't play tennis?"

8

The first world (g) -

JUDGMENT DAY

Captain Alexei Klyuyev was preparing his Tu-134 for approach to Kuibyshev airport in the former Soviet Union when a foolish idea occurred to him.

As the cockpit voice recorder later showed, Klyuyev started boasting to his crew that he was such an intuitive pilot he could land the jet BLINDFOLDED.

Just two minutes before touch-down, he ordered the flight engineer to close the blinds of the windscreen.

Klyuyev opened the blinds a few seconds later just as his aircraft started crashing into the ground.

Sixty-two people died. Klyuyev is serving a 15-year prison sentence.

Something similar ruined the old world. It had fallen into the hands of men who were out to do their "own thing".

If we are to believe the ancient records, they had decided to "go it alone", guided by their own intuition. "Be independent," was the cry. "You don't need a Higher Power to guide you."

So mankind pulled down the blinds on its Creator. They were in rebellion.

That's what the ancient records say.

…And eventually there was a mess.

The nations of this planet Earth were in chaos. They had reached an impasse. No way out.

AGREEMENT ON TEN PRE-FLOOD
GENERATIONS

An interesting point of similarity between the ancient traditions is the statement by many of them concerning ten kings (or fathers) who lived before the Flood.

- In *Genesis* chapter 5, ten successive "fathers" are listed from Adam to Noah. Then, it tells us, the Great Flood came.
- The Sibylline books of *Babylon*, as well as *Hindu, Chinese* and *Phoenician* traditions, agree that there were ten generations before the Flood.
- The *Egyptians* preserved a list of ten pre-Flood "gods".
- The ten "kings" of the *Maya* (Central American) tradition refer to the same period.
- The "Kish King List" of ancient *Sumeria* likewise referred to "the ten kings who lived before the Flood."
- Plato wrote of ten kings of Atlantis before it disappeared under the water. Could this be a memory of the same pre-Flood world?
- A "Stone Age" culture discovered during the late Middle Ages on the *Canary Islands* still maintained the ancient tradition of ten kings.
- The natives of *Greenland* preserve the tradition that ten generations of men had lived upon the earth when a universal Flood came and the whole human race was destroyed.

It is significant that these ten antedeluvian generations recur in the traditions of so many ancient peoples so widely separated in both time and place. They recur with a most stubborn persistency. They evidently have a common source in the same historical facts.

TWO DIFFERENT DOUBLE LISTS AGREE

The book of Genesis states that mankind polarised into two basic groups before and until the time of the Flood. The first group (Adam to Noah) continued for ten generations. The second group (the line of Adam's son Cain) occupied eight generations.

Sumerian tradition likewise preserved two lists of "kings" who reigned before the Flood. One of them contained eight names (as does the family tree of Cain), the other ten names (as does the family tree of Genesis 5.)

```
1 ┬ 1          1 ┬ 1
2 ┴ 2          2 ┴ 2
3 ┐            3 ┐
4 ┼ 3          4 ┼ 3
5 ┼ 4          5 ┼ 4
6 ┬ 5          6 ┬ 5
7 ┴ 6          7 ┴ 6
8 ┐            8 ┐
9 ┼ 7          9 ┼ 7
10 ┴ 8         10 ┴ 8
```

Genesis   Sumerian
list   list

"EXAGGERATED" TIME PERIODS

In the Babylonian history of the ten antedeluvian kings, the obviously overstated "reign" of each king (one, for example, is said to have reigned for 64,800 years) raises immediate doubts. It seems dubious that the highly civilised and intelligent Babylonians could believe such a figure. Yet, modern scholars have attributed such nonsense to them.

However, recent research has shed light on this problem. The Babylonian unit of measurement, the *sarus*, had two different values - (1) the astrological (corresponding to a time period of 3,600 years) and (2) the civil (corresponding to 18½ years).

When this is understood, the problem evaporates.

One need only divide the reign of each Chaldean pre-Flood king by 3,600 to arrive at the basic number, then multiply it by 18½ to obtain the writer's intended meaning.

As Rene Noorbergen explains:

"The changes brought about through this method are so startling that in some cases the so-called reigns of the legendary Chaldean kings become almost identical with the important highlights in the lives of the Biblical patriarchs; that is, the birth of their eldest sons.

"More important, however, is that this new approach boils down the total reign of the ten antedeluvian kings to 2,221 years instead of the hundreds of thousands of years mythology ascribes to them - and this brings the new Chaldean figures of pre-Flood years believably close to the approximate number of years the Bible ascribes to the time that expired between Creation and the Flood....

"Due to the fact that Hebrew figures represent some very peculiar translation problems creating a number of minor deviations in the numerous Bible translations, the Biblical time span that lapsed between Creation and the Deluge is given in at least three different figures.

"The Samaritan version of the early Bible books gives a total of 1,307 years before the Flood. The Masoretic text, on which the King James Old Testament is based gives a total of 1,656 years. The Septuagint version gives a total of 2,242 years.

"Compare the Septuagint total with the Chaldean account of 2,221 years, and we arrive at a difference of 21 years - a breath of years that is almost negligible." [1]

nterestingly, the Toltecs of Mexico believed that the Flood came "after the world had existed for 1,716 years." [2]

In the sixteenth century, the Indian savant Ixtlilxochitl in his *Relaciones* penned a history based on all available pre-Conquest records and legends, aided by his ability to understand the native tongue and decipher the hieroglyphics.

he history began with the creation of the world by the supreme god Tloque Nahuaque. This first era lasted 1,716 years, until floods swept over the earth. This is only a 60 year variation from the figure given in the King James Bible.

POPULATION

In Genesis, it is said that men *filled* the earth.

The possession at that time of a far greater *vitality* of body and mind than we have now would encourage a prolific human population.

The climatic conditions of that original world, the abundance and accessibility of food supplies, of virgin soil and unlimited riches beckoning man to take possession: these were the most *ideal conditions* for population growth.

We cannot be certain as to the world population when the disaster struck. But let's do a little calculating.

On a worldwide basis, five children per family is today considered average, with a female reproductive capacity of say, 30 to 35 years.   Until recently, up to eight or a dozen children was considered the norm in many countries.

Certainly the very much longer life spans in the antedeluvian world must have facilitated a rapid population explosion. If the reproductive capacity of the pre-Flood woman was half her age (as is so for mothers today), then it would appear that 400 years of child-bearing per woman may not have been unusual.

On this basis, a family of 20 to 26 children does not seem unreasonable. Let's be conservative, and allow a family of just 20 children. If, as the ancient sources agree, there were ten generations of mankind up to the Flood, the population developed may have been something like this:

Generation 1	2
2	20
3	200
4	2,000
5	20,000
6	200,000
7	2,000,000
8	20,000,000
9	200,000,000
10	2,000,000,000

his is a figure close to the world's population about 90 years ago.

If we were to assume that antedeluvian families averaged 22 children, then the figure increases to almost 5 billion - the population just a few years ago.

Population figures change rapidly. In the early nineteenth century world population reached 1 billion; in 1930 2 billion; in 1960 3 billion; in 1974 4 billion; in 1987 5 billion; and in 1995 6 billion.

World population grew very slowly until 1650, but then increased from 545 million to 2.5 billion in 1950. By the mid 1980s it had reached about 4.5 billion - and is now in excess of 6 billion.

For a time, one generation simply "added" to the previous one. It is only comparatively recently that the "adding" has been replaced by "multiplying".

And the "multiplying" has produced an exponential growth curve.

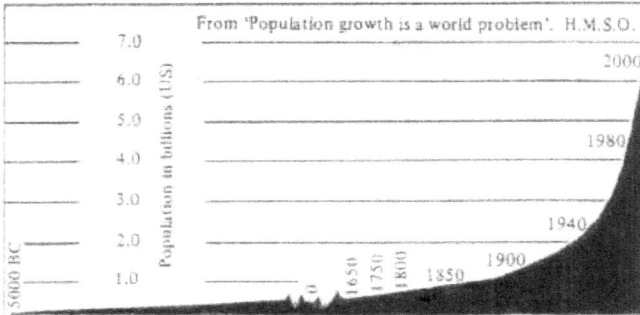
From 'Population growth is a world problem'. H.M.S.O.

The Genesis record refers to a similar state of affairs shortly before the Flood intervened. It says that mankind "began to multiply".[3] Is this how the pre-Flood population graph might look?:

With a likely high birth rate and low death rate in that antedeluvian world, the strong possibility emerges that mankind covered practically the entire globe.

Pre-Flood population might easily have been as great as that of today - or more. It could easily have "filled" the earth, as Genesis says.

INTELLIGENCE

I think it was Albert Einstein who said that man uses only about ten percent of his mental capacity, that we have ten times more brain potential than we'll ever use.

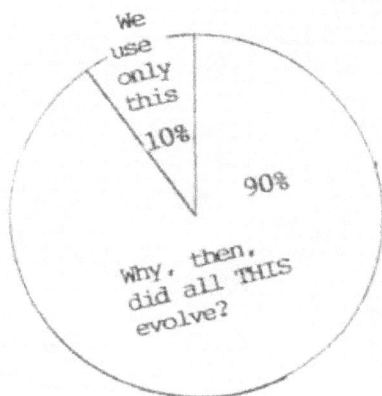

May I toss in a cat among pigeons? If evolution theory were true, then why on earth is the 90 percent of our brain capacity even there?

According to traditional evolutionary theory, body parts are supposed to evolve because of a need for them. This 90 percent makes sense only in terms of original need and use.

So if intelligence really were increasing, the brain would be increasing in size and complexity over the generations - the human brain would not possess, as it now does, large areas which are dormant, or nearly so.

Whilst there is some evidence for a physical degeneration of mankind, it appears that the greatest degeneration has occurred within human intellectual capabilities.

Since our brain has the capacity to store information many times greater than is actually utilised, the human intelligence potential seems, in fact, to have been designed for a creature with a *much longer life span* than we possess today. If the human brain was meant to be utilised to a far greater extent than it is at present - even if it did not use its *full* potential - then the individual would necessarily have had a far longer life span than he does, to obtain the fullest possible benefit from such extra intellectual ability.

We might reasonably assume that the first man possessed the ability to use the entire capacity of his brain.

HIGH CIVILISATION

Did you know that nearly all the writings of ancient peoples worldwide tell the same story, that of a decline from an original "Golden Age"?

Just think of it! With longer life spans and vastly greater brain power - augmented by knowledge imparted by the Creator - the pre-Flood race must have been capable of scientific and inventive reasoning far beyond our present capacity.

There is now evidence that the earliest races did create a civilisation vastly superior to our own.

I used to be a skeptic concerning this. We are taught by evolutionary "history" that early man was primitive. The story goes that we ascended to our present civilised state by a slow, uninterrupted development.

However, twelve years of specialised research, as well as on-site investigation of the FACTS, ultimately compelled me to face this truth: that there was an original advanced world which gave impetus to all succeeding civilisations.

There are recently discovered artefacts that cannot be dismissed, namely objects of metal sitting in museums, unquestionably made in the ancient world, that would have required very advanced technology to produce. A technology not to be repeated until our day.

The weight of evidence grows daily - evidence that all the major secrets of modern technology were known, and forgotten, long ago. Evidence that early mankind did create a society that surpassed ours in all aspects of development.

Could ancient man really have produced such things as earth-orbiting satellites and computers? In my book *Dead Men's Secrets*, the lid is lifted on more than one thousand surprising discoveries - from the seafloor, jungles and desert sands of our planet. There are forgotten secrets that almost smack of science fiction. The evidence is fascinating, even startling!

An ancient Vedic manuscript discovered in India, *The Samarangana Sutrachara*, devotes over 200 pages to describing how to build and fly wingless aircraft. It deals with no less than 49 types of "propulsive fire" used in these vehicles. Some systems used electrical or magnetic forces, others the power of heated mercury.

Other ancient documents, the *Mahabharata*, the *Ramayana*, and *Drone Parva*, also give accounts of these "Vimanas" and their abilities.

With ancient man's incredible mental faculties, tremendous advances were made, advances that you and I can't even begin to imagine.

Because of the difference in the mental capacity between us and the antedeluvians, their civilisation may have followed a very different path from ours. It may have contained elements that are incomprehensible to us and excluded much of what we consider essential.

After the Great Deluge, as the physical earth changed and life spans shortened, human intelligence would deteriorate rapidly - yet not before some super civilisations sprang up. But, as it turned out, their secrets would soon be lost.

REASON FOR THE GREAT FLOOD

A fatal circle of influences ruined the old world. Ancient records are adamant that the basic cause of the Deluge event was spiritual – that it was a judgment on man's wickedness.

We read that crimes unknown to the law, never before seen in the world, were rife. Science was leading the way. Experimenters, by altering the created genetic codes of humans and animals, were creating monstrosities. There was corruption of man and beast.

Two groups were polarising: the Sethites who preserved and respected the original laws given by the Creator of the planet; and the Cainites who were obsessed with materialism and raw pleasure. The Cainites were haughty and shrewd. As intervention approached, they had just about conquered the minds of the Sethites. The number of faithful was diminishing at an alarming rate.

Finally, those that stood out were confined within the narrow limits of a single family group.

Unless there was intervention, there would soon be no survivors.

It is recorded that "the wickedness of man was great in the earth, and… every imagination of the thoughts of his heart was only evil continually." [4] The human race had become almost totally depraved. [5]

And "the earth was filled with violence." [6] A beautiful world was transformed into a house of destructive madness. The balance of nature and the very existence of life on earth was in doubt.

Men like Enoch spoke up loudly that a day of reckoning lay ahead. Noah tried to save his contemporaries from the coming disaster. Few listened.

There are hints, however, that some elite groups took his warnings seriously enough to propose an evacuation from Planet Earth. Allegedly, sanskrit texts in the University of the Punjab tell of space flights 3000 BC. According to Dr. Ruth Reyna (who was commissioned by U.S. Space authorities), these flights were considered imperative **due to the threat of a coming Deluge on earth**.[7]

On the brink

Human life on this planet was poised to blast itself to extinction. It was time for supernatural power to intervene.

A cleansing of the planet would prepare it for future generations. So it was that the surface of the entire earth was now to be disturbed, refitted as a more austere and less bountiful home, where a rebellious race would be better off with less ease and abundance, in an environment not conducive to longevity.

For this new start, an untainted family was spared. They were to be rewarded with life in a new world free from the present human threat.

The destruction of the original earth is portrayed by ancient traditions as a sovereign act of the Creator.

Natural laws were to be the agency. Created forces already latent in nature were to be released for a season. These forces would act according to known laws of hydrostatics and hydrodynamics.

So it happened. Suddenly it struck … a disaster neither man-made nor ordinary. Various natural agencies were suddenly orchestrated on an unnatural scale. And when you consider all the evidence taken together, it does hint at some Intelligence involved.

Just a handful of people lived to see both worlds. The records tell us that they already knew WHEN it would occur and they had been preparing for 120 years.

THE FIRST WORLD – Summary

CLIMATE   Geology testifies to a once mild and uniform climate over the entire globe. There is reason to believe that this paradise world existed within the memory of the human race.

SURFACE   Most of the earth's surface was then land. There were no high mountains forming physical or climatic barriers. Ocean beds were relatively shallow.

PLANTS AND ANIMALS   There was luxuriance of vegetation, pole to pole. Plant and animal types were of greater variety than today. They were also more widely and evenly distributed – and of greater size and quality – than their modern descendants.

VAPOUR CANOPY A vapour envelope surrounding the planet not only precluded winds, storms and rain, but also filtered out life-shortening cosmic rays.

LONGEVITY Several factors favoured a much longer human life span. Indeed, while ancient records recall such longevity, modern science admits to its possibility.

POPULATION   Expansion over some two millennia may have produced a population comparable to our own, sufficiently large to cover the earth.

SCIENCE AND TECHNOLOGY   With the incredible mental faculties of man at that time, tremendous scientific advances were made, advances that we can't even begin to imagine.

CORRUPTION AND VIOLENCE   Yet mankind was sliding into spiritual bankruptcy. Corruption was widespread. Violence was exploding out of control. The race may have become totally extinct, had not supernatural power intervened.

PARALLEL WITH TODAY   Population   explosion   –   a
proliferation of science and technology – worsening corruption –
exploding violence. Does that sound familiar?

INTERVENTION   Suddenly the great disaster struck.   It was
neither a man-made accident, nor an ordinary calamity. It appears to
have been an intelligently directed event, in which vastly different
natural agencies were suddenly orchestrated on an unnatural scale.

9

Flood traditions (a) -

WORLD IN SHOCK

Red sunrise. Breathtaking sunrise over the valley.

The early morning haze and reflection combine to turn the image into one of awesome beauty, like an atomic bomb mushroom cloud.

The atmosphere is eerie and powerful.

There is no sound anywhere. No birds or animals and no people.

Splintered branches poke up from the ground. A muddied shoe, a man's size, leans against some small rocks. A chewed-up book cover. Half an enamel jug.

The emptiness and silence of this place called Earth is almost scary.

… She keeps staring. She almost expects someone to pop around a corner, but no-one does.

Here they are, just eight people left alone on an empty planet.

Empty? Not quite. Countless corpses lie strewn from New Zealand to Norway.

A devastated planet. But only one year ago…

She chokes back a sob. Hardly knowing what she does, Amoela stumbles back inside the survival vessel.

She's shivering uncontrollably. Her husband Japheth holds her close. They both weep.

THE MOST DEEPLY-ROOTED OF ALL TRADITIONS

The Great Flood was known to all peoples of antiquity. The tradition appeared in sunny Egypt, Greece and Australia, in mountainous Peru and Mexico, in icy Greenland and the sandy Gobi.

Tim La Haye and John Morris list 204 Flood traditions from widely separated parts of the world. [1]

But the original mirror of the story has probably been shattered into some 600 pieces. In each broken fragment the object can be seen. It is more distinct in some fragments than in others.

Over time, these traditions have been modified, transformed in the retelling. For example, over time, geographical locations became uncertain.

But, stripped of their accumulated and sometimes fantastic embellishments, there is almost complete agreement among them all on the essential facts of the great catastrophe.

The legends are still just enough dissimilar to offer convincing proof of a shared memory.

Says Hugh Miller, noted Scottish geologist:

"There is, however, one special tradition which seems to be more deeply impressed and more widely spread than any of the others. The destruction of well-nigh the whole human race, in an early age of the world's history, by a great deluge appears to have so impressed the minds of the few survivors, and seems to have been handed down to their children, in consequence, *with such terror-struck impressiveness* that their remote descendants of the present day have not even yet forgotten it." [2]

When Alexander Humboldt, the famous nineteenth century naturalist, penetrated new regions of South America unknown to the Old World at the time, he discovered tribes of wild natives. "And yet among these forgotten races of the human family, he found the tradition of the deluge still fresh and distinct; not confined to a single tribe, but general among the scattered nations of that great region." [3]

Humboldt concluded that "the legends had their origins in *a firmly-rooted, racial memory common to* all men." [4]

Of course, the thought is devastating, but could it be that our modern concepts of earth's history are in need of revision?

CONTENT OF FLOOD LEGENDS

It may be of interest to glance at a few of these Flood traditions. For each main point, we shall cite the common biblical record, followed by a sampling of the world's racial traditions.

Rebellion of mankind

"And God saw that the wickedness of man was great in the earth... only evil continually ... and it grieved his heart. And the Lord said, I will destroy man whom I have created from the fact of the earth... I will destroy them with the earth." [5]

- *Egypt*: Nu, the ruler of the seas, set out to wholly destroy mankind who was in rebellion.
- *Bolivia*: A great Flood was sent to punish men's pride and insolence.

In most of the legends around the world, the reason for the catastrophe is the same.

A divine warning

"And God said unto Noah ... Make thee an ark... with thee [8 persons] I will establish my covenant." [6]

- *Iran* (the Zend Avesta): Yima was ordered by a god to prepare for a world deluge.
- *India*: Manu, the father of the human race, was instructed to build a ship and take in seven others (total 8), plus all the different seeds. The waters reached the mountains.
- *North America* (Great Lakes): After a warning of the coming deluge, the hero built a vessel for his family and the animals. They floated for several months.
- *Sumeria* (Gilgamesh tablets): The hero was warned of the coming deluge and built a vessel lined with pitch.
- *U.S.A.* (Yuchi Indians of South Carolina and Georgia): A big flood drowned all but those who had been warned of the impending disaster.

A survival vessel: man and animals

"Come... into the ark... Of every clean beast thou shalt take to thee by sevens, the male and his female, and of beasts that are not clean by two, the male and his female. Of fowls also of the air by sevens, the male and the female: to keep seed alive upon the face of all the earth." [7]

- *Alaska*: The father of the Indian tribe, warned in a dream that a deluge would desolate the earth, built a raft on which he saved his family and all the animals. They floated on the water for several months.

- *Australia* (Aborigines): The flood survivors used rafts and canoes and carried birds and animals.
  - (Aborigines): A rainbow serpent came down when a great flood was supernaturally sent because of man's wickedness, and told 8 people to climb on board its back so that it could save them from this flood.
- *North America* (Iroquois): One family was saved, with two animals of each kind.
  - (the Thlinkeets): Several people survived the deluge by seeking shelter in a great floating building. [8]
- *Greece*: Lucian, in his account of the Greek traditions, speaks of the ark and the pairs of different kinds of animals. [9]
- *India*: The animals were taken on board the boat to escape the great flood. [10]
- *Mexico*: (Toltecs): Men were destroyed by tremendous rains and lightning from the sky, and even all the land, without the exception of anything, and the highest mountains were covered up. A few escaped from this destruction in a "tpotlipetlacali" (a closed chest).

Other undisputed sources of antiquity considered the Flood to be not local, but a worldwide event.

The name "Noah"

"And Noah did according unto all that the Lord commanded him." [11]

- *China*: The Chinese ancestor Nu-Wah survived the destruction of the world by a flood and accomplished the reconstruction. There followed legendary heroes sometimes referred to as the Three Sovereigns (Noah's three sons?). After these came the Three Dynasties, Hsia, Shang and Chou (held by scholars to initiate the historical period).

- *Venezuela*: In the Sierra Parima between Brazil and Venezuela, there is reported to be a dead city called by the name of Ma Noe, signifying "the waters of Noah."
- The name Noah has survived for thousands of years, through a multiplicity of stories, even though oft times it evolved into a slightly different spelling, depending on the letter symbols used. This is remarkable, when you consider the wide separation across the earth, as well as the ultimate language differences between peoples, and the extreme local distortions which developed in Flood legends. Yet the same name survived virtually unchanged in such widely separated places as
- Hawaii (where he was called Nu-u)
- the Sudan (Nuh)
- the Amazon region (Noa)
- Phrygia (Noe)
- Africa (Noh and Hiagnoh – among the Hottentots)
- Egypt (Nu)
- Turkey (Nuh)

8 survivors

According to the biblical story, *8 people* survived – Noah and his wife, their three sons, and their three wives. [12]

- *Hawaii*: When Kane decided to destroy the earth which man's wickedness had spoiled, he allowed Nu-u, the Righteous Man, to escape by building a great canoe with a house on it. He was told to take on board his wife, 6 other people *(total 8)* and all the animals he wanted, to await the great flood. The rains came, the oceans merged and all mankind perished. Eventually, as the waters subsided, the rainbow became a token of forgiveness, and Kane told Nu-u and his three sons to repopulate the earth.
- *Mexico:* An old Toltec myth speaks of all the world drowning, *except 8* men who escaped in a house like an enclosed ark. They called it "Tlapitlipetlocalli", and painted it on their rolls as a small boat with an awning on top, and 8 heads peering out. [13]

85

- *China:* In a Chinese Flood story, the hero escaped the destruction, together with his wife, three sons and three daughters. ***Total 8.***

And here is a fascinating aspect of ancient Chinese writing. It contains words that can be traced only to "Nu-Wah" and the Flood.

For example, the ancient character for "ship" (still printed in Chinese books and papers) is composed of the pictures for "boat and "8 mouths", suggesting that the first ship was a boat carrying eight persons. [14]

VESSEL + EIGHT + MOUTH = BOAT

From a study of the Chinese ideographic system of relaying written information, it is clear that there were thought to be eight survivors within both words for the Ark and the Flood itself.

EIGHT + UNITED + EARTH = TOTAL .... + WATER = FLOOD

Noah's "three sons"

The biblical account speaks of Flood survivor Noah and his three sons, Japheth, Shem and Ham. [15]

- *India:* The hero of the Flood had three sons – Iyapeti, Sharma and C'harma. (Compare these names with Japheth, Shem and Ham.)
- *Greece:* Homer, in his *Iliad*, shows us that the Greeks likewise recollected three brothers. The Greeks trace themselves back to Japetos. (Compare that with the biblical Japheth.)
- *China:* The Chinese Flood survivor likewise had three sons.

Time of the year

"…in the second month, the *seventeenth day of the month*, the same day were all the fountains of the great deep broken up, and the windows of heaven were opened." [16]

The season of the year in which this fearful event destroyed the human race was later commemorated worldwide. That season was the New Year festival, observed at the disappearance of the Pleiades, at the end of October or early November. (The first month of the ancient year fell in October, not January as it does today.)

Davidson and Aldersmith have made precise calculations and conclude that the *17th day of the second month* of Genesis corresponds to either *October 30, 31, or November 1*, of our Gregorian calendar. [17] The Genesis year began at the Autumn equinox, in the Northern Hemisphere.

The festival at this date was one of the most universal of all customs. It was observed in connection with *THE MEMORY OF THE DEAD*, or as a feast of the ancestors.

At this time of the year, the memory of the dead was observed by
- the Aborigines of Australia
- savages of the Society Islands
- the Hindus
- the Irish
- the Persians
- the Celtic Druids

and in places as WIDESPREAD as
- Mexico
- Egypt
- Fiji
- France
- Peru.

The DAY OF THE DEAD (our Halloween) was a commemoration of the MASS DISAPPEARANCE OF A LARGE PART OF THE WORLD'S INHABITANTS.

Specific examples

- In Mexico, *"the festival of the dead"* was held on *November 17*. They had a tradition that, at that time, *the world had been previously destroyed*. And they dreaded a repeat of it. [18]

87

- In Egypt, the 17th *day* of the Egyptian month Athyr, or Hathor (our November) was identified with the Festival of the Dead. In Egypt, Hathor was considered the "angel of death" and was associated with the destruction of the earth by water.

  It appears that, originally, the 17th *day* of the *second month of the original pre-Flood year* was commemorated as the 1st day of the 1st month of the early Egyptian Calendar year. (That is, they calculated their new year from the date the Flood had begun.)

  But as time went on, the persistence of the tradition connecting the festival of the dead with the 17th day of the month, led to the adoption of the alternate Egyptian dating. *Thus November 17 became an alternate date to November 1.*

  This alternate dating (*November 17*) was used by certain cults in *Egypt* during Dynasties XII and XIX, in Ptolemaic Egypt.

  On this day, a priest would place an image of Osiris in a *sacred ark* and launch it *into the sea*, to disappear from sight. [19]

- The date *November 17* also occurred in *Rome* as an alternative date to November 1.

- The *Hindus* celebrate "Durga", a *festival of the dead*. This was originally their New Year's Day and it was celebrated on *November 17.*

- The month of *November* was, in *Persia*, formerly called "The Month of the Angel of Death." They celebrated the *feast of the dead* at this time.

- In *Australia*, Aborigines celebrated the *festival of the dead* in November, when the Pleiades is most distinct. This constellation was specifically worshipped as "THE GIVER OF RAIN."

We have noted that the correct anniversary of the Flood was either October 30, 31 or November 1 (although the fact that this was the "17th" on the old pre-Flood calendar did lead to celebrations on November 17, as well).

Worldwide, however, the FESTIVAL OF THE DEAD is associated with a date generally ranging from October 31 (All Hallow's Eve, or Hallowe'en) to November 2 (the modern All Souls).

These traditions shared a common remembrance of the dead, which seems to commemorate some major calamity that overtook the human race. There are echoes of a perishing world and the rebirth of another.

A definite connection appears to exist between this worldwide festival and the biblical record that the Great Flood began about the beginning of the ancient New Year (October-November): "... in the second month, the *seventeenth day of the month*."

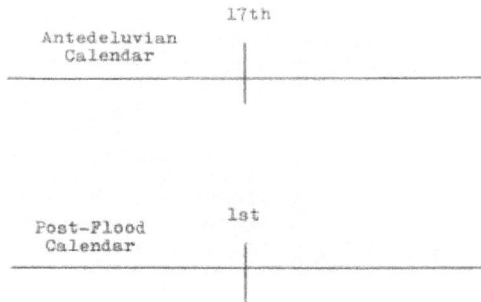

```
                                17th
        Antedeluvian
         Calendar                |
_____|_____
                                 |



                                1st
        Post-Flood
         Calendar               |
_____|_____
                                 |
```

The year

In a previous work [20] I dated the Flood and the rise of Egypt with its post-Flood sister civilisations, too early. At the time, I noted (page 349) that the month and day were more accurately determined. But the year, I suspected, could be subject to revision. New evidence confirms that this suspicion was well founded.

According to the exhaustive research done by Davidson and Aldersmith,[21] the common astronomical chronology of the Hebrews, Egyptians and Babylonians defines that the Deluge occurred from 2345 to 2344 B.C.

The astronomical chronology of the Hebrews and Egyptians defines that the Deluge began on November 1 (Gregorian calendar) and officially terminated on November 11 the following year.

Davidson argues strongly that the independent histories of Egypt and Babylon can now be synchronised perfectly at all points of contact with the biblical history of Israel and even earlier dates can be correlated back to before the Great Flood.

Chinese dates likewise make sense when compared to the Genesis account.

In China it is told that a tremendous flood of devastating force occurred in approximately 2300 B.C.

The Chinese sacred book of the Shu-king, translated by W. Gorn Old, speaks of Fu-hi. Notice the similarities to the Genesis record:

The Bible	*Book of Shu-king*
When Noah emerged from the Ark, God used a rainbow as a sign of his new covenant with the human race. *(Genesis 9:13-17)*	Fu-hi was "born of a rainbow."
Noah saved in the Ark seven of each type of clean animal: from these he offered a sacrifice after the Flood. *(Genesis 7:2; 8:20)*	Fu-hi bred and saved 7 kinds of animals to be used as a sacrifice.
Noah was born 600 years before the Flood. *(Genesis 7:6)*	The Epoch of Fu-hi began in 2944 B.C. (600 years before 2344 B.C.)

Locations of some of the 600 worldwide Great Flood traditions

Earth's axis tilted

- *Eskimos*: The earth tilted violently before the Flood began.
- *Mexico*: "The earth shook to its foundations. The sky sank lower towards the north. The sun, moon and stars changed their motions. The earth fell to pieces, and the waters in its bosom uprushed with violence and overflowed.... The system of the universe was totally disordered. Man had rebelled against the high gods. The sun went into eclipse, the planets altered their courses." [22]
- *China*: The earth tilted violently before the Deluge. The sky suddenly began to fall northward. The heavenly bodies changed their courses after the earth had been shaken.
- *Egypt*: The earth turned over. [23]
- *Greenland* (natives): When the Great Flood came, the earth capsized like a boat.
- The *Polynesians* and *Hindus* also related this phenomenon.

Earthquakes

- *Rome* (Ovid, the poet): In the great Flood the earth "shivered and shook" as the gods made "an end to the race of men." Soon "there was no telling land from sea."

Underground basins burst forth

- *Mexico*: The earth fell to pieces and the waters in its bosom uprushed with violence and overflowed.

(Compare this with the biblical description: "the fountains of the great deep were broken up.") [24]

Volcanic action

Less universal than the Flood legends, though not less striking, are the reports of a Great Fire which swept the earth as part of the great cosmic catastrophe.

Covered the mountains

The Genesis account states: "… and all the high hills, that were under the whole heaven, were covered… and the mountains were covered." [25]

- *Sumatra* (the Battacks): The last human pair were knee-deep atop the highest mountain before the Flood subsided.
- *Celebes* (the Toradjas): The Flood covered the highest mountain, until the only creatures that escaped were a pregnant woman and a pregnant mouse.
- *Peru*: A terrific explosion and the world was plunged into darkness. Water rose to the height of the mountains.

- *Guatemala* (Maya): Amid earthquakes and fiery eruptions, it rained tar with water. Then day became black night. Even the mountains disappeared under water.
- *North America* (the Athapascan): "Every day it rained, every night it rained… The sky fell, the land was not… The waters of the oceans came together. The waters completely joined everywhere… Trees and grass were not… Human beings and animals alike had been washed away… It was very dark." [26]
  - (Hopi): "Waves higher than mountains rolled in on the land and continents broke asunder and sank beneath the sea." [27]

- *South America* (Guarani Indians, east coast): The hero rode on a palm tree till mountains disappeared. Only when the waters touched the sky did the Flood stop. A heavenly bird beat its wings as a sign that the waters were abating.
- *China*: The waters, "…in their vast extent, over-topped the great heights, threatening the heavens with their floods." [28]

Duration of the Flood: a year

- *Romania*: Gypsies tell the "tale of the fish": An old man was warned, "Put your wife and family in a big boat to save yourself, for this rain will continue for a long, long time. Make room in the boat for animals and plants as well, for everything that is touched by the great flood will die. All creatures will die in the flood." The floods continued to soak the earth for a year. Nothing but sky and water was seen. Even the birds had perished. When the rain stopped and the waters had abated, a full year had passed. When they left the boat, they found a different world waiting. Eternal life was no more. The old civilisation had vanished. Labour and sorrow, sickness and death, were now close.

(Compare the biblical dates, showing that the Flood survivors were inside the Ark for a year.) [29]

Birds sent out

The Genesis record says: "And the waters decreased continually until the tenth month: in the tenth month, on the first day of the month, were the tops of the mountains seen. And it came to pass at the end of forty days, that Noah opened the window… And he sent forth a raven, which went forth to and fro, until the waters were dried up from off the earth. Also he sent forth a dove from him, to see if the waters were abated from off the face of the ground; But the dove found no rest for the sole of her foot, and she returned unto him into the ark, for the waters were on the face of the whole earth: then he put forth his hand, and took her, and pulled her in unto him into the ark. And he stayed yet another seven days; and again he sent forth the dove out of the ark; And the dove came in to him in the evening; and, lo, in her mouth was an olive leaf plucked off: so Noah knew that the waters were abated from off the earth. And he stayed yet another seven days; and sent forth the dove; which returned not again to him any more." [30]

- *North America* (the Arapaho): The entire planet was covered by water, until Arapaho ordered three ducks to dive down and bring up some dirt, whereupon the waters began to subside.
- *Greece*: The gods warned of a great flood because of man's wickedness. A survival boat was built. It ultimately rested on a high mountain, and a dove was sent out twice.
- *Cuba*: "An old man, knowing the deluge was to come, built a great ship and went into it with his family and abundance of animals; and… wearying during the continuance of the flood, he sent out a crow, which at first did not return, staying to feed on the dead bodies; but afterwards returned bearing with it a green branch." [31]

- *Mexico*: In the universal Flood, only one man saved himself in a spacious vessel with his wife, children, animals and grain. Later he sent out a vulture from the craft. Feeding on the carcasses which covered the earth, it did not return. But a humming bird flew back with a leafy branch. So, aware that vegetation was resprouting, the hero disembarked on a mountain.
  - another legend even mentions the dove that did not return, because it had found dry ground.
- *Chaldea*: A history compiled by Berosus, a Chaldean priest, from Chaldean records and traditions relates details of the Great Flood. Xisuthras, the tenth king, was warned in a dream to build a ship, enter with his family and dearest friends, as well as provision it with food and drink, animals and birds. Toward the end of the Flood, in which all men died, he sent out some of the birds. These, finding no food or resting place, returned to the ship. Some days later, he sent them out again; this time they returned with their feet full of clay. The third time he released them, they returned no more. Xisuthras thus learned that the earth was bare. From an opening in the ship's roof he then saw that it had rested on a mountain. Disembarking, the company raised an altar and sacrificed to the gods. A voice told them that the country where they were was Armenia. Of the ship, portions still remain in the mountains. From the ruins, pilgrims scrape asphalt, which is used as a preservative against magic.

Rainbow seen for the first time

The Genesis account states that God told Noah and his three sons: "I do set my *bow in the cloud*, and it shall be for a token of a covenant between me and the earth…[that] the waters shall no more become a flood to destroy all flesh." [32]

- *Hawaii*: Finally, after leaving the *rainbow* as a token of his eternal forgiveness, Kane made the waters subside and told Nu-u and his three sons to repopulate the earth.

- *Guatemala:* "And the *rainbow* appeared in the sky signifying that all below had been destroyed" [33.]
- *Australia:* Many Aboriginal tribes have their Flood stories in which many people die, and the *Rainbow* Serpent is often associated with these Flood myths. In the Aboriginal Dreamtime myths, the serpent has the strange ability to control floods and rain. This stems from his connection with the one world Deluge. The Serpent's appendix *"Rainbow"* certainly suggests that this is correct and automatically dates the creation stories of the Dreamtime with the Great Flood, as no rainbow is known earlier than this event.

The rainbow is fairly well represented in most sources of mythology.

If the pre-Flood world was watered by a mist, and if this situation prevailed until the time of the Great flood, then the rainbow would be unknown until the first rain fell at the time of the Deluge. Until that event, the meteorological phenomenon of the rainbow was something unprecedented in the skies of our ancient earth.

As the rainbow is not mentioned until after the Flood, it is the indelible link and insoluble tie between the events of mythology and the Flood.

10

Flood traditions (b) -

A CANNIBAL'S TALE

"They won't eat YOU!" laughed Dr. Pat Hannan. "You're not salty enough."

My health clearance in hand, I was about to leave for the Cannibal Isles.

A hundred years ago that term would have been more accurate. For centuries travellers avoided the fearful Melanesian islands of the South Pacific, where shipwrecked men were eaten.

Of course civilisation had come to the islands and cannibalism was a thing of the past… almost.

It was reported that a few newly discovered tribes still ate the flesh of their departed.

One could mention the Samo-Kubo tribe. Deep in the almost impenetrable jungle of western Papua New Guinea lived this hitherto unknown tribe. Yes, they were cannibals. They had almost no contact with the outside world.

But, relevant to the subject of our previous chapter, they had preserved in essence the same biblical Flood story. Here's how they tell it:

Due to someone teasing the lizards, the Lizard Man caused a worldwide Flood, which drowned all except two brothers and a wooden vessel.

The story features animals, a mountain, and the theme that from the survivors of that worldwide Flood came today's world population.

The tribe's remoteness and the interweaving of the story with its very cultural essence appear to ensure that there has been absolutely no contamination from outside sources.

The concept of a Golden Age, or a Paradise World, destroyed in a great disaster, usually described as the work of the gods, is so widespread and deeply rooted in human mythology that it almost appears to be a piece of instinctive knowledge in the collective human subconscious.

COMMON AGREEMENT

There is common agreement among Flood legends on numerous points. Even after allowing for the ultimate embellishment with local colour and culture, the similarity factor between these legends remains remarkably high.

We have already noted some of these:
- A favoured family (in 88% of the stories)
- Who were forewarned (in almost every tradition)
- Survival due to a boat (70%)
- Animals also saved (67%)
- The Flood being worldwide (95%)
- The survivors ending up on a mountain (57%)

So many of the traditions agree that an *animal or bird* was sent out to *explore*. Even the *olive leaf* is remembered. Some legends recall in striking and precise terms the appearance of the *rainbow* as a token after the Deluge, a *"thanksgiving" sacrifice*, and specific reference to the survival of an *eight-member family*. Sometimes even the *number of days it rained* coincides, varying from the biblical 40 days to 60 in some American Indian versions.

They agree that the Flood was an exceptional cosmic disturbance.

ORIGINATED WITH MISSIONARIES?

The Flood story, as we have noted, is universal. It is known even among out-of-the-way tribes who have had no contact with the outside world – thus could not have acquired it from others.

Anti-Flood theorists have objected that missionaries must have been responsible for introducing the Flood story to such remote tribes. And, on the surface, that sounds plausible enough. But then, when you think a little deeper, a few, straight questions begin to come up.

For example, if it was missionaries who brought the Flood story, then why are not other biblical stories also found in the folklore of such tribes? Why not stories like Jonah and the whale, or the biblical destruction of Sodom and Gomorrah, the parting of the Red Sea and other miraculous stories found in the Bible?

And why is it that *the only traditions found* among isolated tribes are those that relate to the VERY EARLIEST events – namely, creation, the fall of man into sin, the Flood, the Tower of Babel and the confusion of languages? In other words – only those stories *said to have occurred before the scattering of man*? But NOT those events which occurred AFTER the scattering of the nations.

On the other hand, if the nations and tribes truly began to disperse to remote places ONLY AFTER THESE EVENTS (as the Bible claims) then should we not expect them to have taken with them the memory of these earlier events, which they indeed do hold - but not the knowledge of later events?

And another question.

If missionaries are responsible for the similarities in Flood accounts, then who or what is responsible for the differences? Differences which include time-corrupted details like the roused anger of the Lizard Man, distortions which could not have been passed on by anybody knowledgeable of the biblical story.

And something else. Missionaries, so it turns out, have in the past never reached all these remote tribes of the world. Even if they had, they certainly would have focused on the Christian gospel rather than concentrating all of their teaching upon the Genesis Flood.

In fact, there is on record the experience of a missionary who, relating the story of the Flood, was interrupted by the natives who wanted to tell *their* version of the same story!

The truth is, MOST OF THESE FLOOD TRADITIONS HAVE BEEN GATHERED BY ANTHROPOLOGISTS OR PENNED BY UNBELIEVERS who had no interest in vindicating the biblical account.

They have, to their surprise, discovered such traditions in tribes which no missionaries had ever reached.

WHY, THEN, DO THESE TRADITIONS EXIST?

Suppose there were NO FLOOD LEGENDS… could not this very lack of circumstantial evidence be used as a powerful objection to the veracity of the biblical account?

On the other hand, if there actually WAS a Flood that destroyed mankind, then worldwide traditions should be EXACTLY what we would *expect* to find.

This much is sure. Peoples all over the world "remember" the Flood. It has left an indelible impression on the memory of the entire human race.

In an analytical comparison of all these hundreds of traditions, historical data can be perceived. These worldwide traditions make it crystal clear that this Great deluge was no mere Mesopotamian Flood. A universal catastrophe MUST HAVE taken place. To deny this is to reject the most ancient and common traditions of universal mankind.

The eminent scholar William Wundt, who could never be accused of a biblical bias, and tried his utmost to prove the independent manufacture of the various Flood traditions, was forced to admit:

"Of the combination of all these elements into a whole [the destruction of the earth by water, the rescue of a single man and seed of animals by means of a boat, etc.], however, we may say without hesitation, IT COULD NOT HAVE ARISEN TWICE INDEPENDENTLY." [1]

Could it be, then, that every man and woman alive is a direct descendant of the Ark survivors? Could it be that, as they migrated in groups from the landing spot, they carried the memory of this traumatic event?

A UNIFIED CONCEPT AT THE START

Also fresh in their minds was the concept of a Creator who had intervened in human affairs.

Research by Oswald O. Tobisch has shown that rock drawings scattered over Asia, Europe, America and Africa are related to each other. (and we can now add Australia to that list.[2] Tobisch asks in amazement:

"Is it possible that once there was a united concept of God on an international scale simply inconceivable to our present way of thinking and that mankind in those days was still in the 'field of force' of the 'primordial revelation' of the one and almighty creator, to whom mind and matter, the whole universe with the heavenly bodies and living creatures, were and are subordinate?" [3]

THE STORY UNDERGOES CHANGES

Over centuries of separation, the story of man's common past was adapted to each changing culture, but the essence remained the same.

These legends of a worldwide Flood are compelling evidence that the global catastrophe as recorded in Genesis is ONE OF THE GREATEST FACTS OF ALL HISTORY.

It has been claimed by at least one writer that the Flood legend was unknown to the Egyptians. This raises the question, could this mean that the Flood did not reach Egypt?

Sorry, that writer was mistaken. In the ancient papyri, it is recorded that a person called *NU* was the begetter of the very gods of Egypt. I ask you, how much closer could this be to the biblical *Noah*? (See the variations of Noah's name in the preceding chapter.)

Nu was one of the original EIGHT (8) gods of the Egyptian pantheon. These eight were considered to be gods by having passed through and survived a judgment. They were also considered gods because of their longevity, which their offspring did not inherit to the same extent. Here are the hieroglyphics:

Nu is directly connected with the *watery mass* (note the waves that help to make up his name); from this watery mass the gods came "in the bark" (the Ark?).

The *eighth* member of this company of gods was *Set*. Set occupied a place in the boat when they came from the waters at the creation (or dawning) of a new age. Set is called *"son of Nut"*. The *Nut* would be Noah's wife, the *Nu* in the feminine gender, or the goddess who accompanied Nu on the voyage. Nut, as the mother of all living (as was Nu the begetter of the Egyptian gods in the masculine sense), was held in esteem among the gods and remembered as Isis.

	áp - tu	mut - k	Nut	en	átef - k	Nu
Nut	Is decreed	thy mother	Nut	to	thy father	Nu

Interestingly, *Shem* (Set?) was the son of Noah and his wife. In Hebrew, Shem'i-nith literally means *"the eighth."* [4]

It would require a struggle not to see here the connection with the Flood as a perceived historical event on the part of the Egyptians.

SOMETHING FOR THE SKEPTIC TO CONSIDER

Who experienced the Great Flood? Certainly all mankind alive at that time. And a handful of them survived to pass on the tale from one generation to another.

But later, people refused to accept the accounts as describing a real event and laughed them away as fairy stories.

The *ancient* author – living within a few hundred years of the events he describes (or else even writing as a contemporary) – *is far more likely to be in secure possession of the facts* than a skeptic of the 21st century who is separated from the event by 4,000 years or more.

GENESIS COMPARED TO OTHER ACCOUNTS

It has been common for critics to "put down" the biblical book of Genesis as a collection of fables copied from other ancient sources.

However, internal evidence shows it to be head and shoulders above every other record of the Great Flood.

(a) Not spoiled by "local" colour

For example, whereas many tribes "relocated" their landing place to the nearest high mountain, to add impact to their Flood story, the biblical record did not.

The Genesis account states that the Ark landed "upon the mountains of Ararat." [5]

This reference to "the mountains of Ararat" is significant, since the Hebrews had no personal knowledge of that distant land. This testifies to the integrity of the biblical account.

(b)   Older than other Middle Eastern reports

Critics have tried to establish that the biblical account had no historical authority, but, rather, that it was borrowed from the well-known Babylonian legend. It is commonly asserted that the book of Genesis was written as late as the 6th century B.C.

This view shows an unawareness of the latest modern discoveries.

It has now been substantiated that the Bible record is the oldest of the Flood reports of the Middle East.

The Bible account *includes archaisms* which indicate that it preceded the Babylonian and Assyrian versions of the Flood.

One of the greatest archaeologists of all time is Professor W.F.Albright. He points out that the archaic features contained in the Genesis record date it before any Mesopotamian version that is "preserved in cuneiform sources"

Babylonian tablet describing the Flood events

(such as the Babylonian "Epic of Gilgamesh" and the Assyrian "Epic of Atrahasis"). [6]

Further evidence comes from archaeological sites excavated comparatively recently, such as Ebla in Syria. Tablets from Ebla, dated to 2000 B.C. show records of the past which are parallel to those in early Genesis. These show that the biblical stories did not stem from Babylonian legends originating around 700 B.C.

(c) The purest version

Contrary to what was once claimed, it now turns out that the Bible account cannot be the second-hand one. It is infinitely superior. The biblical book of Genesis tells a *simpler, more coherent* story. It does not bear the marks of the superstitious, the magical or the grotesque, which occur in the Babylonian and Assyrian versions. These latter bear the marks of later distortions, clearly inferior to the Genesis account.

An example is the specifications of the Ark. The Babylonian/Assyrian Deluge account gave the ship a rather flat description. In lines 57 through 61, the Gilgamesh Epic states that its floor space was one "iku", a measurement which has been translated to mean 3,600 square metres or approximately one acre. It reads, "One iku was its floor space, one hundred and twenty cubits each was the height of its walls; one hundred twenty cubits measured each side of its deck." This leads to only one conclusion – the boat was an exact cube!

This would make it a crudely designed cubic vessel with the tendency to keep turning with each gust of wind as if caught in a gigantic whirlpool.

Contrast that with the description in the book of Genesis. From a point of stability and rolling, its ratio of six to one (300 cubits by 50) is about as perfect as can be desired. Some of the giant tankers have a ratio of 7:1. In modern engineering terms, the Genesis specifications are of perfect proportions; in this they bear the stamp of an accurate transmission of up-to-date sophistication. (We shall see evidence of this in a later chapter.)

Something else. The Genesis account contains a detailed family genealogy extending from the time of the Flood down to the historical Moses. And this leads me to ask, is it not fully consistent to hold that a family tenacious enough of its traditions to preserve its genealogy from Shem to Moses, could have handed down its own account of so memorable an event?

Notice what some other researchers have discovered.

Kenneth Kitchen of the University of Liverpool, comments:

"The common assumption that the Hebrew account is simply a purged and simplified version of the Babylonian legend (applied to Flood stories) is fallacious on methodological grounds. In the Ancient Near East, the rule is that simple accounts or traditions may give rise (by accretion and embellishment) to elaborate legends, but not vice versa. In the Ancient Orient, legends were not simplified or turned into pseudo-history (historicized) as has been assumed for early Genesis." [7]

La Haye and Morris concur:

"It almost goes without saying that the beautiful story handed down, likely in written form, from Noah through the patriarchal line, finally to be incorporated into the book of Genesis by Moses, *stands in a class by itself when compared with other versions for meaningful transmission of information.* If the universal law of cause and effect has any meaning at all – that is, that the effect cannot be greater than its cause – then there can be no doubt that the less accomplished writings and tales of secular historians are merely corruptions of the original and meaningful Genesis story." [8]

Between the Gilgamesh Epic and the Bible account, there are a number of important *differences*. Alexander Heidel has carefully analysed these. He concludes that even though there are definite similarities, these areas of agreement are apparently caused by the two stories having been based on the same *event*, NOT the same account. [9]

* * * * * * *

It seems strange that the tradition of a Flood would last for so long among so many diverse nations of the world, if it were not based on an actual event. *There have been many floods on this planet and most of the stories associated with them are soon vanished.* But the central theme of the worldwide Flood has survived, leading us to suspect its authenticity.

LOGICALLY, IT BOILS DOWN TO THIS: THE BIBLICAL FLOOD RECORD CAN BE ACCEPTED BY INTELLIGENT PEOPLE, SO LONG AS THEY BELIEVE THE BASIC FACT OF A CREATOR WHO WOULD INTERVENE IN THE AFFAIRS OF HIS CREATURES.

FLOOD TRADITIONS – Summary

DEEPLY-ROOTED   The destruction of well-nigh the whole human race, in the remote past, by a Great Flood, was known to all peoples of antiquity.

Hundreds of Great Flood traditions have survived. These are from widely-separated parts of the world that were not in communication with one another within historical times.

COMMON AGREEMENT On the essential facts of the catastrophe, there is almost total agreement among all races everywhere.

From the combination of elements in each legend it soon becomes clear that the same story in its details could not have arisen twice independently.

DIFFERENCES   Nevertheless, the traditions are just enough dissimilar to offer convincing proof of a shared memory – before the original dispersion.

THE BIBLICAL ACCOUNT COMPARED   Archaisms in the biblical record (as found in the book of Genesis) establish it as the oldest of the Great Flood reports of the Middle East. Another significant comparison: it is remarkably free of the embellishments which mar the other Flood records. Hence the Genesis account can be considered a meaningful transmission of information concerning the event.

A REAL EVENT   The worldwide persistence of traditions concerning the Great Flood of the Bible leads us to judge the Bible record as authentic. It also suggests that the great Flood is one of the greatest facts of all history.

11

Worldwide flood (a) -

THE FLOOD THAT
NEVER REALLY WENT AWAY

She slumped on to the kitchen floor in a spreading pool of blood.

Hank suddenly realised his mistake. It was not to him that his housekeeper had raised the knife; she had been about to cut down the overhanging meat – to prepare it for the roast.

Well, he wouldn't be arrested. He had a government licence to kill. Anyway, he'd killed over forty blacks already. One more wouldn't matter.

Only twenty-one, Hank van Loenan was a seasoned, stony-faced, cynical mercenary.

When I met him at the backpacker's hostel, he was taking time off to see the world. I was in the hostel lounge room, conversing with a Maori.

Somehow the conversation had drifted to the subject of this book.

I looked up. The South African's eyes were blazing.

He grabbed the Maori by the shirt and roared, "Come on, nigger, I don't want you in here!"

There were a few awkward moments while several of us in the room intervened.

Hank then turned on me. His eyes were mocking.

"Oh," said he. "So you believe that nonsense!"

"We were talking about Noah's flood," said the Maori. "It does make sense."

THE GENESIS FLOOD "MYTH"

"Noah's flood?" he spluttered, trying to suppress a laugh. "You can't take that story seriously. It's just a tale for children. It doesn't fit into history."

"So the biblical Flood is pure fiction?"

"Well, not quite," said Hank. "Perhaps there was some sort of flood. Just a local one. It probably occurred in the Mesopotamian valley. And so we got our myth of Noah's flood."

At this stage of the story, perhaps it wouldn't hurt to look at this biblical "myth". It's recorded in the first book of the Bible, known as Genesis (Meaning "Origin").

It relates that the Creator observed how mankind had become vicious and depraved. He informed a just man by the name of Noah that He had decided to destroy all mankind. Then He instructed Noah to build a boat with three decks; the length of the vessel to be 300 cubits (515 feet); its width to be 50 cubits and its height 30 cubits.

Taylor paraphrases the account as follows, beginning with verse 17 of chapter 6:

"Look! I am going to cover the earth with a flood and destroy every living being – everything in which there is the breath of life. All will die. But I promise to keep you safe in the ship, with your wife and your sons and their wives. Bring a pair of every animal – a male and a female – into the boat with you, to keep them alive through the flood. Bring in a pair of each kind of bird and animal and reptile. Store away in the boat all the food that they and you will need. And Noah did everything as God commanded him.

"Finally the day came when the Lord said to Noah, 'Go into the boat with all your family, for among all the people of the earth, I consider you alone to be righteous. Bring in the animals, too – a pair of each, except those kinds I have chosen for eating and for sacrifice; take seven pairs of each of them, and seven pairs of every kind of bird. Thus there will be every kind of life reproducing again after the flood has ended. One week from today I will begin forty days and nights of rain; and all the animals and birds and reptiles I have made will die.'

"So, Noah did everything the Lord commanded him. He was 600 years old when the flood came. He boarded the boat with his wife and sons and their wives, to escape the flood. With him were all the various kinds of animals – those for eating and sacrifice, and those that were not, and the birds and reptiles. They came into the boat in pairs, male and female, just as God commanded Noah.

"One week later, when Noah was 600 years, two months, and seventeen days old, the rain came down in mighty torrents from the sky, and the subterranean waters burst forth upon the earth for forty days and nights. But Noah had gone into the boat that very day with his wife and his sons, Shem, Ham, and Japheth, and their wives. With them in the boat were pairs of every kind of animal – domestic and wild – and reptiles and birds of every sort. Two by two they came, male and female, just as God had commanded. Then the Lord God closed the door and shut them in.

"For forty days the roaring floods prevailed, covering the ground and lifting the boat high above the earth. As the water rose higher and higher above the ground, the boat floated safely upon it; until finally the water covered all the high mountains under the whole heaven, standing twenty-two feet and more above the highest peaks. And all living things upon the earth perished – birds, domestic and wild animals, and reptiles and all mankind – everything that breathed and lived upon dry land. All existence on the earth was blotted out – man and animals alike, and reptiles and birds. God destroyed them all, leaving only Noah alive, and those with him in the boat. And the water covered the earth 150 days.

"God didn't forget about Noah and all the animals in the boat: He sent a wind to blow across the waters, and the floods began to disappear, for the subterranean water sources ceased their gushing, and the torrential rains subsided. So the flood gradually receded until, 150 days after it began, the boat came to rest upon the mountains of Ararat. Three months later, as the waters continued to go down, other mountain peaks appeared.

"After another forty days, Noah opened a porthole and released a raven that flew back and forth until the earth was dry. Meanwhile he sent out a dove to see if it could find dry ground, but the dove found no place to light, and returned to Noah, for the water was still too high. So Noah held out his hand and drew the dove back into the boat.

"Seven days later Noah released the dove again, and this time, towards evening, the bird returned to him with an olive leaf in her beak. So Noah knew that the water was almost gone. A week later he released the dove again, and this time she didn't come back.

"Twenty-nine days after that, Noah opened the door to look, and the water was gone. Eight more weeks went by. Then at last the earth was dry. Then God told Noah, "You may all go out. Release all the animals, birds and reptiles, so that they will breed abundantly and reproduce in great numbers.' So the boat was soon empty. Noah, his wife, and his sons and their wives all disembarked, along with all the animals, reptiles, and birds – all left the ark in pairs and groups.

"Then Noah built an altar and sacrificed on it some of the animals and birds God had designated for that purpose. And Jehovah was pleased with the sacrifice and said to himself, 'I will never do it again – I will never again curse the earth, destroying all living things, even though man's bent is always toward evil from his earliest youth, and even though he does such wicked things. As long as the earth remains, there will be springtime and harvest, cold and heat, winter and summer, day and night.'" [1]

* * * * * * *

"Hank," I called, "perhaps you can help me. Suppose someone asked you, how would YOU answer these questions?"

"Write them down," he replied. "Then I'll consider them."

…After lunch, we met in the lounge room. "Got them?" he asked. I handed him a sheet of paper.

"Mmm," he said, scanning them quickly. "See you soon," and retreated to his room.

JUST A LOCAL FLOOD?
These were the questions:
1. Why would Noah spend more than a century building a vessel just to escape a local flood? Why couldn't he just move?
2. If it were only a local flood, then why would Noah spend a century of planning and toiling, in constructing a huge ship to accommodate two of every known species to escape it? Could not those animals have been led out of the doomed valley to the nearest hills as easily as they were led to the Ark?
3. Even if all the animals in the Euphrates valley were destroyed, were there not enough outside the valley to perpetuate their species?
4. Why were birds taken into the Ark? Are we to be so credulous as to believe that birds would not be able to fly away from the rising waters of a single valley?

5. Does it not border on the ridiculous that Noah should be divinely commanded to build a boat nearly half the length of the "Queen Mary" simple to float up and down that one flooded valley?

6. Could Noah have been so ignorant of the topography of southwestern Asia as to think that the Flood covered all the high mountains "under the whole heaven" when, as a matter of fact, it covered only a few foothills?

   The double statement "*all* the high hills, that were under the *whole* heaven, were covered"[2] is practically equivalent to a Hebrew superlative. It leaves no doubt that the writer is saying that the Flood covered the earth's entire surface.

7. The Bible says that water covered the planet for *150 days*, and took *a further 7 months* to subside sufficiently for dry land to appear.[3] Even if the mountains were only hundreds of feet high, a twelve month flood could not pile up and remain in one local spot. Wouldn't gravity cause the water to find its own level and cover the whole earth?

8. If the Ark finally landed thousands of feet up in the mountains of Ararat, as the story says, how could that happen in a mere local flood?

9. The stated purpose of the Flood was to wipe out a degenerate race. The entire human race outside the Ark was to be destroyed.[4] Their sin was not regional, but universal. The race was so utterly corrupt morally, and of all mankind only a handful were to be spared because they did not go along with the great sin drift. The Bible record is emphatic that Noah and his family were the only ones to escape.[5] "*All* flesh... under heaven... every living substance that I have made will I destroy from off the face of the earth." Destroying only a local portion of the race by a local flood – how would that have served the stated purpose?

10. According the record, God told Noah, "I will destroy them *with the earth.*"[6] Another passage says that "*the world* that then was, being overflowed with water, perished."[7] If not only all men, but *the earth also* were to be destroyed, wouldn't the Flood obviously have to cover the earth?

11. According to Genesis, God promised there would be "no more such a flood again."[8] So if Noah's was only a local flood, then how do we explain all the other "local" floods that have occurred

since? Millions have perished in vast and destructive *local* floods in many parts of the earth.

For example, the aftermath of the 1883 Krakatoa explosion caused   flood waters which destroyed 300 towns and villages with 36,380 people. Those flood waters rose 120 feet high.

The 1876 Gulf of Bengal hurricane aftermath would have to be called a deluge. A flood wave 35 feet high swept across 141 square miles of land, drowning 215,000 people.

After the Thera disaster about 1470 B.C., which swept across Mediterranean countries, Moses would have had to record that God had broken His word.

…UNLESS THERE WAS **ONLY ONE** GREAT FLOOD. AND THERE HAS BEEN NOTHING LIKE IT SINCE.

The whole Genesis account becomes ABSURD if the Deluge was not worldwide.

PERHAPS THEY THOUGHT THEY WERE THE SOLE SURVIVORS?

I did not see Hank again until that night. He looked thoughtful.

"I have *one* answer to all your questions," he grinned. "Probably they **thought** it had been a total world wipe-out. Perhaps they **thought** they were the sole survivors."

"Nice try," I smiled. "But, tell me, Hank, how likely is that… really? Floods happened so frequently in Mesopotamia that one has the clear impression of a society that had come to terms with them, rather than regarding them as something so special that they gave the survivors the impression that they were the only beings left on earth. No, my friend. This Flood of Noah was SOMETHING DIFFERENT.

"Legends of a Flood that had swept over the WHOLE world, covering hills and even mountains – these legends are distributed worldwide. Ancient peoples must have been as vulnerable to tropical storms, snowstorms, tornadoes and other seasonable disturbances as are we. Surely they would not have been impressed by the mere overflow of a river to such a degree as to carry their experience to all parts of the world as the story of a cosmic upheaval."

"I hate to admit it," said Hank, "but that's a hard one to answer."

Hank sat by the window. Headlights from a turning vehicle blinded him for a flash. He shielded his eyes.

"But there's a problem. A serious one. You won't convince me."

"Go on."

NOT ENOUGH WATER FOR A
GLOBAL FLOOD?

"Look," continued Hank, with a skeptical lift of the eyebrows. "There's not enough water on earth to make a worldwide Flood. Do you realise, Jonathan, that if all the clouds over the earth emptied themselves simultaneously, the earth would not be covered by even one foot of water?"

"Yeah. A real problem," I repeated.

"Well, is that all you say?"

"Not quite."

"I don't see how you can wriggle out of that."

"You want facts?"

"Sure… FACTS. If you can. But I don't like your chances." Hank was enjoying this.

Great, I thought. He's ready.

"Let's start with the ice stored on top of Greenland and Antarctica," I began. "If only those two masses were released, the sea would rise by 150 feet."

"Sure, that would drown thousands of towns and cities," quipped Hank. "But not the mountains. You still don't have enough water."

"Agreed. Now, about 71 percent of our globe is covered by water and 29 percent is dry land. The area of the Pacific Ocean alone is nearly 10 million square miles greater than ALL the continents and islands added together."

I paused for a drink. The room was crowded. Some were watching television; others, I noticed, were reading or playing cards.

"Go on," urged Hank.

"Did you know, Hank, that the average depth of the ocean is 13,000 feet – and the average height of the land is only 2,300 feet? So the ocean is, on average, 5½ times deeper than the land is high. That means there is about 18 times more water below sea level than there is dry land above it. If all the land now above the sea were dumped into the ocean depths, it would fill only one eighteenth of the oceans.

Sea water volume is 18 times land volume

"Again, if all the land were smoothed out (no mountains, no ocean basins), the water would completely cover it to a depth of 1½ miles – 7,800 feet of water over the entire surface of the earth."

"Whew!: exclaimed Hank. "I never thought of that. But there ARE mountains. And there ARE ocean basins. And there probably always have been. Still doesn't help you."

"Oh yes it does! And here's why. It's an established fact that most of the earth's mountains are of recent formation – in historical times, that is.[9] So very likely, the pre-Flood mountains were not as high as today.

"It is also agreed that sea beds can rise and continents sink. This being so there is no difficulty whatever in finding enough water, even for a universal flood." [10]

"Must go now," said Hank. "Mighty interesting. Let's get into this more, tomorrow. Good night.

SOURCES OF THE GLOBAL FLOOD WATERS

It was a warm evening. Just a breeze. Very gentle. And no mosquitoes, thankfully. So I went outside and sat on a bench.

I'd tell him tomorrow, I thought. That would help. Hank was quite honest. Like many intelligent folk, who don't know the facts, he'd just assumed the Flood was a myth, and that was it. Yet it was the biggest single heritage event that our whole human race shared in common.

Yes, I'd let him know tomorrow. Let him know that the water which produced the global Flood originated from THREE SOURCES.

Think I'll share that with you now. Briefly, of course.

114

1.   Underground basins

Huge amounts of water were locked under the earth's crust. These were "broken up" as the Deluge began.[11]

According to tests, "there is an additional, virtually inexhaustible supply of 'primary' water that is independent of rainfall. Like the geologists' juvenile water, it comes from the depths of the earth. Carried along underground channels, natural pressure forces it upwards towards the surface of the ground, often in places impossible to predict by geological methods. Dowsers perceive this water as flowing through a vast network of vein-like faults in rock, occasionally rising even to the tops of hills in natural pipes, and then spreading out in a dome like the spokes of an umbrella.

"In conventional geology books, there is nothing to support this. Nevertheless, inexplicable sources of water have occasionally been noted." [12]

To their surprise, scientists drilling the world's deepest well near Kola in northern Russia found deep underground large open channels filled with hot, mineral-rich water.[13]

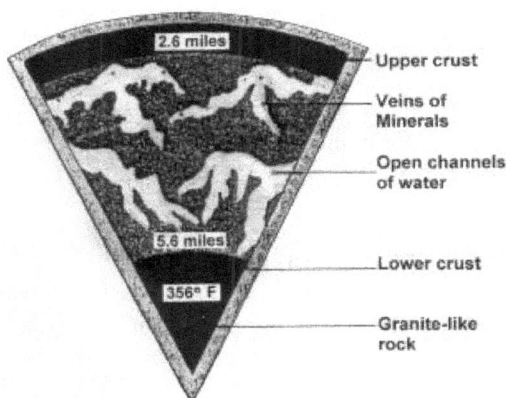

2.   Thousands of volcanoes

When the earth's crust was suddenly shattered (see the second book of this series), perhaps as many as 30,000 volcanoes erupted in unison, each giving off millions of gallons of water a day. Volcanoes expel water vapour as well as cinders.

3.   Water canopy

An antediluvian water canopy enveloping the earth (see Chapter 3) was precipitated at the time of the Deluge. It contained enough water to cascade as torrential rain over the whole earth for six weeks non-stop. It was at this time that these waters entered our present oceans.

This thermal water blanket exists no longer. The great masses of waters which destroyed the world are still lying in the depths of the expanded ocean.

MOST OF THE EARTH STILL FLOODED

Come to think of it, the Flood waters never totally went away.

Before the Great Flood, the proportion of land area to water area was larger, perhaps very much larger, than now. At some time in the past, much of the present sea bottom was dry land. (See Chapter 1.)

Late during the Flood, the crust of the earth was pushed up, raising land and pushing wider the ocean bed to receive the run-off water. This water covers large areas that, before the Great Flood, were land.

So it may be said that the waters of the Flood still lie over large portions of the earth.

Who doesn't love the sea, watching the waves race in, one after another, toward the shore, hearing them crash, seeing them splash over the rocks!

Now, whenever I am on a boat I gaze out over the restless blue... and ponder.

At least 30 percent of this huge mass of water was added as a result of the Great Deluge. Down there, under the boat, is land where people once walked and breathed. I am looking at the waters of Noah that never went away.

Can you imagine those men and women of Noah's day? Undoubtedly there were many who protested, "There's not enough water on earth to produce a worldwide Flood." And they had more reason to say that than do we.

12

Worldwide flood (b)

WHY HANK GASPED

The next morning as I sat under a tree, Hank plopped himself down and said brusquely:

"It had better be good… where's the evidence?"

"Do you have an hour?"

"Sure. Let's go up to my room and you can lay out your diagrams on the floor."

Hank found the global Flood a problem, simply because it didn't fit the evolutionary theory we'd all been taught at school.

I'd prepared some cardboard pieces that illustrated the evidence he needed to see.

FOSSILS SHOW SOMETHING ELSE

First we covered the fossil evidence. He saw it laid out… startling indeed. The fossil *facts* did ***not*** show a progressive development of life forms from simple to complex, as the evolution theory leads us to expect. Not at all! Surprise of surprises.

As says Stephen Jay Gould, Professor of Geology and Paleontology, Harvard University, "The evolutionary trees that adorn our textbooks have data only at the tips and nodes of their branches; the rest is inference, however reasonable, ***not the evidence of fossils***." [1]

Hank fidgeted uneasily. The fossils buried in the planet's surface showed SOMETHING ELSE. (And just what they do show will be investigated in Book 2 of this series, *Surprise Witness*.)

Now we came to a turning point. And here were some of the facts that came to mind:

IF A GLOBAL FLOOD DID OCCUR...

1.   Traditions   If a global Flood did occur, there should be many cultural traditions of the flood story. There are.

2.   Sediments   If a global Flood did occur, we should expect thick water-laid sediments to form most of the surface crust of the earth's land area. And they do.

You see, sedimentary rock is WATER-LAID ROCK – laid by silt deposition as moving waters slow down. Of the earth's land surface, 75 percent is covered by sedimentary rock. Which means that the major factor in the formation of the present surface of the earth has been *water movement ON A GLOBAL SCALE.*

Do you get that?

The very structure of the rock strata reveals that the earth's surface must have been torn up for miles down and relaid by the action of water. In some places there is evidence that it occurred as far as ten miles down!

The earth's crust has been CHURNED into a mass of water, vegetation, animal life and rubble.

This is *prima facie* evidence that the entire surface of the earth has, indeed, been under water fairly recently.

And something else. Professor M.E. Clark, University of Illinois, and Dr. Henry Voss have formulated a model which shows the global sedimentary context formed by the effect of the moon on the waters of a theoretical global Flood. The academic impact is this: There is evidence of a global Flood – and there is a global association in the laminated layers of sedimentary rock. There is intercontinental linking evidence which shows a global Flood occurred before the continents were separated.

3.   Mountains covered   If a global Flood did occur, we should find evidence on mountain tops. We do.

The fact that sedimentary rock covers not only the lowlands, but also the mountain peaks, shows that not only was the water movement global, but that it also extended above the tops of the mountain ranges.

And crests of mountains contain marine fossils. Evidently the mountains were once under water.

4.   Rapidly buried remains   If a global Flood did occur, there should be buried remains of all manner of life forms found mixed up in the sedimentary layers. There are.

All over the earth are extensive fossil graveyards which show evidence of sudden catastrophic burial and rapid lithification. To put it simply, rapid, violent burial and fast turning to stone.

The uncovering of death pits of all types of animals (land and sea animals MIXED TOGETHER) in areas throughout the earth points *not* to a *local but* a *general* event.

5. Human relics buried at all levels If a global Flood occurred, we should find so-called "higher animal" skeletons (including man) at many different depths in the flood-produced rocks. We do. (See the astonishing evidence in Book 2 of this series)

COULD SUCH PHENOMENA HAVE BEEN CAUSED BY A SERIES OF LOCAL FLOODS?

The following six phenomena raise interesting questions:

1. Pressure and force Today, local floods are not known to be able to generate the type of tremendous pressure and force necessary to fossilise creatures in rock.

2. Grand Canyon The majestic Grand Canyon, with strata clearly laid down by water force, and packed with millions of fossils, is too gigantic for its cause to have been a local flood. On that point, there is compelling evidence that the strata of the Grand Canyon was clearly laid down by water force. That the Grand Canyon sandstone containing footprints was not deposited by wind, but by a catastrophic event involving water on a grand scale.[2] There will be more on this subject in the 3rd book of this series.

3. No worldwide inter-face There is no worldwide surface between any two geological formations.

Popular theory teaches that the land received its carcasses then sank under the sea for deposits of silt, etcetera, to bury them. After this, it arose to become land again. This cycle was repeated many times and each time a new layer formed. When an uplift raises the local sediments above water level, depositing stops. The soil build-up resumes and erosion begins. And this becomes a time gap – or an "inter-face" between two periods of sediment deposition.

BUT!!! There is *no* such worldwide inter-face, *except* at one spot - the very bottom of the strata pile.

Thus there is evidence of *no worldwide time gaps.*

Instead, the whole column (pile) of sediment layers (laid by water) is continuous from bottom to top.

NOW! Combine this with the fact that *every layer* in the column *was formed rapidly and catastrophically.*

THIS MEANS THAT *the entire worldwide column of layers with its fossils was formed RAPIDLY AND IN QUICK SUCCESSION, layer upon layer.*

I know this will upset somebody, but I have to say it. Our pet theories need to be overhauled!

Yes, it is true that there exist many local unconformities in local geological sites, but it is now known that there is no worldwide unconformity, except, as we noted, at the very bottom of the column.

The evidence that each layer was formed rapidly is derived from the fact that a single fossil may penetrate through several layers. Often such a fossil is well preserved. Which means the sediment layers formed around it *rapidly*, before decomposition could take place.)

4.   Coal beds Everyone knows how coal seams form. Trees grow in a swamp, die, fall over, and are buried by sediments, finally turning into coal, right? Wrong! Coal seams do not form that way.

There is no way that the vast coal beds on earth could have been laid down that way.

For example, in Australia there is a continuous coal seam from south of Wollongong, in New South Wales, to north of Brisbane in Queensland. This seam is 800 miles (1,250 kilometres) long, and up to 200 miles wide and very thick. Some swamp!

Trouble is, most of the trees in this coal seam are conifers, in other words, pine trees. When is the last time you saw a pine tree growing in a swamp? Pine trees do not grow in swamps.

Nor can a mere local flood explain it.

We're looking here at 1,250 kilometres of forest catastrophically buried by water! What kind of *local* catastrophe could explain sudden burial on that sort of scale? (Bearing in mind that professional coal geologists today would acknowledge that coal *had* to form by rapid burial.)

5.   Pillow lava   In the lava rocks of the earth's strata are "pillows" – clear evidence that the volcanic layers were formed under water.

6.   High water-level marks   All over the world are marks of a former high water level in lakes and rivers – ancient high beaches and high river terraces. These testify to the time when a flooded planet was being marked by a receding flood level, as the waters drained back into the newly enlarged ocean basins.

There are indications of enormous, canyon-cutting flow-offs through the soft, flood-laid strata.

Every modern river is an "under-fit" stream, far too small to have produced its own canyon and valley sections or the extensive beds of alluvium through which it flows.

Practically all the earth's crust consists of sediments or sedimentary rocks obviously laid down under moving water (except for the few formed by ice or wind after the sedimentaries). This indicates that the whole surface of the earth has been under water fairly recently. In fact, 70 percent of the earth's surface is still under water. Even the mountain ranges are known to have been uplifted recently, geologically speaking.

The argument that 33 different Noah's Floods would be needed to produce our known coal beds, will be answered in Book 2 of this series: *Surprise Witness*".

UNPARALLELED VIOLENCE

The Great Flood...   We are speaking of an event that encompassed volcanic and tectonic activity on an unprecedented scale; as well as tidal waves, hurricanes, continents splitting apart and ocean basins enlarging.

Virtually every geological feature on earth was shaped by this interlinked complex of catastrophes.

It can be argued that the *facts* of geology (as distinct from certain interpretations of the facts) attest to a worldwide flood of water. Earth's scars speak of a catastrophe which is big enough to call our whole evolutionary theory into question.

The truth is, no single explanation except a global Flood can adequately explain all the geological phenomena.

EVERY SQUARE FOOT of the earth's surface must have been profoundly altered.

You and I today are witnesses that Planet Earth's original mild topography and pleasant climate has been replaced by vast oceans, rugged terrains and violent climates.

As Sylvia Baker puts it:

"How lightly we view the Flood! Yet the events of that year affect us still today. The whole climate of the earth was altered; the volcanic and earthquake activity that persists today began then. Man's life span was reduced to one tenth of its former span." [3]

... Hank gasped. "It's THAT important!" he breathed. "Yes, I see it now. That Flood really *did* happen!"

I could see he was as surprised as was I the first time it struck me. Our lives are so different today – SIMPLY BECAUSE THAT EVENT OCCURRED!

For Hank something had changed. He knew it.

A WORLDWIDE FLOOD – Summary

A "MYTH"   The Noah's flood spoken of in the Bible is by many considered to be a myth, a tale just for children.

OR A "LOCAL" FLOOD   At best, the story may have originated in some local Eastern flood, we are told. When one reads the biblical story, however, it soon becomes evident that the writer intended us to believe it was a worldwide event. The details in the Genesis account become absurd if the Deluge was not worldwide.

NOT ENOUGH WATER?   Calculations reveal that there certainly is enough water on earth to produce a flood of global dimensions. Three sources of water were apparently available: juvenile water from subterranean basins, water from volcanoes and water from the pristine water canopy. Such water eventually added to that of our present oceans – which now cover large areas which were once dry land. It could be said that the waters of the Flood still lie over a large portion of the earth.

EVIDENCES FOR A GLOBAL FLOOD   Evidence for a global Flood comes from the many cultural traditions of the Flood, as well as from the very structure of the planet's crust: waterlaid sediments over 75 percent of its surface; the presence of marine fossils on the crests of mountains; and the fossil graveyards all over the world in which land and sea animals are MIXED UP TOGETHER. Additionally, human relics are found in *all* so-called "ages" of strata.

ONE FLOOD OR MANY LOCAL FLOODS?   A series of local floods could not have produced the features seen today in the earth's crust. Only a global Flood can adequately explain all the geological phenomena.

UNPARALLELED VIOLENCE   We are talking about an event that encompassed volcanic and tectonic activity on an unprecedented scale; simultaneous tidal waves, hurricanes, continents splitting apart and ocean basins forming. Every square foot of the earth's surface must have been profoundly altered. The events of that year affect us still today. The whole climate of the earth was altered; the volcanic and earthquake activity that persists today began then. Man's life span was reduced to one tenth of its former span.

Our lives are so different today – SIMPLY BECAUSE THAT EVENT OCCURRED!

13

Noah's Ark questions -

NO ROOM FOR ERROR

"Even God could not sink her," it was said.

After the *Titanic* went to the bottom of the Atlantic Ocean, taking about 1,500 to their death, it was believed that an iceberg had ripped open her side.

Decades would pass before the wreck was located, broken in two, on the seafloor. Then it was discovered that she did *not* go down as a result of her side having been ripped open.

When the passenger liner struck a floating object (the iceberg), the stress was such that rivets holding the hull together popped out, allowing the water to pour in. The ship broke apart and sank two miles down to the seabed in two large sections. These sections were discovered lying 600 metres (2,000 feet) apart.

After an analysis, United States maritime experts concluded that the *Titanic* sank because the hull's metal plates were constructed of low-grade steel that was made brittle by the cold waters of the Atlantic. The result was extensive fracturing, which hastened the sinking of the gigantic vessel.

The analysis suggests that the rumbles and roars heard by survivors on the night of the sinking were caused not so much by shifting gear and boiler explosions as by the fracturing of huge amounts of brittle steel.

When cooled and stressed, some types of relatively primitive steel fracture much like glass rather than bending or stretching as ductile materials do.

The early supertankers, which came into service during the 1960s, were designed as if they were only half or a quarter the actual size. This led to gross miscalculation of the stresses involved – and ship after ship cracked and broke up in heavy seas.

And now, in the twenty-first century, this is still occurring

Carrier Breaks Back

NZ Herald Nov 26 1988

Tanker 'broken in half'

Halifax, Thursday

All 27 crewmembers were missing today after the Liberian-registered oil tanker Oriental Odyssey caught fire, broke in two and sank in the stormy waters of the mid-Atlantic. A Canadian Forces aircraft circled the area, but could find no trace of survivors, officials said. — AFP

In December, 1985, a court of inquiry released its findings. The sinking of the "Hawea", it disclosed, was due to an inherent design fault.

East Timor denial

The Governor of East Timor, Mr Mario Viegas Carrascalao, said tonight he would resign if allegations over the deaths of...

All hands lost

HALIFAX, November 1983

All 27 Greek and Honduran crewmen from the 65,000 tonne British tanker Odyssey with a cargo of one million barrels of oil are missing after the ship broke up and caught fire in heavy seas in mid-Atlantic.

Fire kills 22

But back now to a very ancient vessel – Noah's ship.

...Attended by a screaming hurricane, gigantic tsunamis swept from pole to pole. The surface of the entire globe became as a giant maelstrom, in which continents and seas were churned up together. Outside the survival vessel, man ceased to exist.

While the turbulent convulsions of the Deluge raged around the Ark, inside this stronghold existed another world all its own. For months it floundered on swirling currents, providing shelter and refuge for eight people and representative animal life.

When he built his ark, Captain Noah had just one chance to get it right. There was no opportunity to test it.

If anything had gone wrong, if the stresses had been miscalculated, then that was it! No more human race. Every living thing on this planet was locked up inside that vessel. If the rivets had popped out, if the vessel had broken its back, we were all finished.

There was no room for error...

JUST A SMALL, HELPLESS BOAT?

"I don't believe that Noah's Ark tale, you know," said Hank. "How could all the animals fit into such a small boat? It was probably scarcely larger than an ordinary fishing smack. It would have been helpless before the slightest squall."

I could understand Hank saying that. A friend's little girl once showed me a picture of Noah's Ark in her story book. The giraffe was poking his head out of the window, to ease the pressure I guess. You'd have to admit, that would hardly relieve the problem!

"Good question, Hank," I was pleased to admit. "But I have been going over the claimed dimensions of the survival vessel. They are staggering. You know, according to Genesis the Ark was 300 cubits long, 50 cubits wide and 30 cubits high. It also had three decks.[1] It was, if you calculate it out, longer than a football field. That's enormous. At 20.6 inches to the ancient cubit, it was 515 feet (158 metres) long! [2]

"You work it out. That vessel displaced something like 32,000 tons or more. Do you know, it would take a freight train three miles long to provide the same cubic space?"

TOO MANY SPECIES OF ANIMALS
TO FIT IN?

"All very well," replied Hank. "But aren't there just too many species of animals in the world to have all fitted inside one ship?"

"Well, how many types of animals are there?" I would refer Hank to Ernst Mayr, probably the leading American taxonomist. "Mayr lists 1,072,300 animal species.[3] Sixty percent are sea animals and of the rest seven out of ten are insects. There are less than 20,000 species of land animals (mammals, reptiles, birds, amphibians) living today, with a much smaller number of extinct species known from the fossils.

"Of course, only the representative types would need to be preserved. Take, for example, today's almost endless varieties of pigeons. If they are allowed to breed together, they go back to the rock pigeon. Thus, if there was just one pair of rock pigeons in the Ark, there were thousands of varieties potentially preserved. The same is true of the dog and every other separate group. Just the basic type needed to be preserved, not every variety within that type.

"Now consider that the average size of all mammals is about that of a house cat.

"Using only 41 percent of available space, all the animals could have been stored in the Ark. And remember, most animals could have been placed in cages and stacked in tiers.

"The real question is, What did Noah do with all that spare room?"

Comparison of size

129

WHAT ABOUT HUGE MONSTERS
LIKE DINOSAURS?

"Okay, then," said Hank. "But how could the Ark possibly shelter such ponderous reptiles as the dinosaurs? Like the 19 foot high tyrannosaurus, the 87 foot diplodocus, and the 50 ton brachiosaurus? I assume you believe the dinosaurs were alive at that time? Not that I do."

"A REAL BIG problem, eh?"

"You've said it, mate!"

"Hank, just suppose you were Noah," I replied. "In order to preserve an oak tree, would you need to take a fully grown oak into the Ark? Surely an acorn would have sufficed?"

"Yeah, that makes sense."

"Well, why not with animal specimens, too? Bearing in mind the purpose for preserving them, young, healthy ones were undoubtedly selected, rather than the largest of each species.

"As far as plants were concerned, we may reasonably assume that apart from perhaps a favourite rose bush or two, as well as choice garden and field crops, no plant passengers were taken on board. The whole plant realm had to survive the Flood fury as best as it could outside the Ark."

UNABLE IN ANCIENT TIMES TO
BUILD SUCH A LARGE VESSEL?

"But it's unlikely," responded Hank, "that a vessel of such dimensions could have been constructed in prehistoric times. Large ships are a modern thing."

"Good one, Hank. Firstly the Ark is said to be too small. Now it is too large!," I said, laughing.

"I grant you, just centuries ago shipbuilding techniques were comparatively basic, with size limited, and we have assumed this was always so. The evolution theory teaches us that there was a steady, uninterrupted progression from a primitive state to the sophistication of today.

"But this can't be so, my friend. Medieval Europe was so 'benighted' in nautical skill that, as Harvard professor Barry Fell observes, 'Columbus' whole expedition could mount only 88 men, carried on three vessels of which two were only 50 feet in length, about the size of a small Boston fishing boat. Contrast that with the Pharaohs of the Ramesside dynasty, 1200 B.C., who could mount expeditions of 10,000 miners across the Indian Ocean.'[4]

"Did you know, Hank, that ocean going vessels of the ancient Greeks were up to 600 feet long and could carry crews of 600. Egyptian open sea ships were as long as 350 feet, with as many as four decks. There were ancient luxury vessels containing temples and swimming pools, with dining halls of marble and alabaster, and modern plumbing.[5]

"Whew!" exclaimed the South African. "Is that so?"

"Surprising, isn't it? Seems our earliest ancestors were more capable than their successors. Only one thing can explain the high level of civilisation at the beginning. Those earliest cultures got their heritage basically from the world that was wiped out in the Deluge. They continued where the generation of the biblical Noah left off.

"Ultimately these civilisations entered into decline and gradually the original knowledge was lost. And with the onset of the Dark Ages, the world forgot its past.

"I don't think there can be any doubt, old chap. The technology of the antediluvians (those pre-Flood people) was quite able to produce a vessel of 32,525 tons, or 515 feet in length."

CONSTRUCTION MATERIAL

"But if the Ark was the product of a high technology, then why on earth was it made of wood? Why not of iron or steel?"

"You do come up with some interesting questions, Hank."

"Yes, you count on me." Hank grinned and shuffled. "Now, don't stall, Jonathan!"

"Well, for starters, bear in mind, the pre-Flood world had a free abundance of superior timber. That's for sure. Wouldn't that be reason enough to choose timber as construction material?

"As a matter of fact, the major reason why our largest modern vessels are not fashioned from wood is not because of our advanced technology, but due to the limitation of size imposed by timber."

"Go on, you're kidding."

"Okay, there should be an encyclopedia here. Let's take a look."

We found a copy of *Encyclopaedia Brittanica*, and went searching. Soon Hank came up with this statement:

"Yeah, it says that 'ships made of iron and steel could be *larger.*' [6]

Hank put back the volume and turned to me. "So *that's* why we use iron and steel! It has nothing to do with our technological superiority. Interesting."

"So why was timber used for Noah's survival vessel? Along with everything else in that first world, tree sizes were enormous. That's why he was able to use timber.

"And here's another thing, Hank. Something that stresses the strategic importance of timber to our modern civilisation in the future."

I was opened to an article in another source: "Because it is renewable, is available at relatively low cost, and has such a variety of structural, ornamental, aesthetic, insulating, and chemical properties, *wood* is considered by many mid-20th century observers to be *the most important raw material of the future, exceeding even the metals, oils, and rubber.*" [7.]

"Well, what do you think of that!"

So the use of wood has nothing to do with the superiority or otherwise of a culture.

And there was something else worth mentioning: Wood endures; metal corrodes.

Just suppose it was intended that the Ark should endure not merely through the brief period of the Deluge, but for posterity, then wood was the only material to use.

As the tangible link between the original pre-Deluge world and our own, might it not be too valuable a monument to be destroyed?

If the Ark was older say, than the Pyramids, might not its preservation and eventual discovery constitute the grand climax of all archaeological finds?

It is reasonable that the builders had such preservation in mind.

As to the ability to utilise metal, it should perhaps be noted that, 600 years before the Deluge, metal-working was already a science. [8]

As Genesis records: "To Lamech's other wife, Zillah, was born Tubalcain. He opened the first foundry forging instruments of bronze and iron." [9]

It took our civilisation about 600 years to develop from gunpowder and printing to nuclear physics and computers. How far, do you suppose, must the antediluvians, in a similar period of time - from Tubalcain to Noah – have advanced, before the Deluge struck?

NO PRIOR SEA TRIALS?

Hank was thoughtful. And more questions kept tumbling out of his brain.

"But surely," he asked, "how could Noah ever have built a boat on dry land that would be able to withstand such a tempest as this Deluge?"

"You're right about one thing, Hank. The Ark was built on dry land. And it had to face a global destruction by water *without the benefit of sea trials.*"

"So you see my point, Jonathan. Even in modern times, large vessels that have undergone stringent preliminary tests, have later succumbed to storms."

"Only too true, my friend. But I'll share this with you. Modern maritime engineers have subjected the claimed dimensions of Noah's Ark to critical tests and have come up with results which are startling.

"During World War I, after a ship broke apart, certain engineers went to the Bible to ascertain the Ark's dimensions. The result? They built the *Aquatania.*

"Remember, Noah lived over 4,000 years ago. Until his day, according to Genesis, there had not been any mighty storms.

"Isn't it remarkable, then, that Noah built a ship, which, according to today's knowledge, was of the *best possible dimensions* to survive a storm? And this, not knowing what a storm was!

"This is a vital point to consider, since optimum design has, during this century, been achieved *only from long experience, often after fatal errors.*

"But with Noah's Ark, the stakes were supreme. There was NO ROOM FOR ERROR. There could be NO SECOND CHANCE.

"Now, honestly, Hank. You tell me. Was Noah just stabbing in the dark, or might the blueprint have been given him, as Genesis states?"

Silence. Hank looked a little worried.

Somewhere in my files I recalled a statement by shipbuilding researcher J.W. Rich. So I went searching, later, and found it.

Rich revealed that a number of incidents had "convinced marine architects that a wooden vessel could not with safety be built longer than 525 feet."

He went on to say that "Noah's Ark was just that length."

Then this question was raised, "Was that just a coincidence, or does it reveal a scientific background in shipbuilding? To be properly waterborne the Ark represents the largest possible construction that might with safety go to sea. To be made larger is to be structurally weak, due to the requirements to be met in bridging the waves where the vessel would otherwise be uniformly buoyed. A wood vessel of larger dimension would be unable long to withstand the strain to which it would be subject at sea." [10]

After sharing this with Hank I asked him, "How on earth was Noah aware of this?"

WHAT ABOUT STABILITY?
Wouldn't this greatest of
tempests have capsized it?

"But surely", objected Hank, "if that cataclysm was as violent as you say, then the Ark would surely have been in danger of capsizing as tidal waves moved rapidly back and forth across the earth. Those inside could not have survived such conditions for a year."

"Hey, I love the way you think so deeply!" I quipped. 'You're dead right, that Ark had to be invincible. It would have to endure the roughest, most violent sea storms that would ever strike this planet. Any modern typhoon would be like a child's breath compared to this year-long nightmare.

"But Hank, whoever worked out the specifications for the Ark must have known this. You see, the Ark ratio of 6 x 1 (300 cubits by 50) is, from the point of view of stability and rolling, about as perfect as can be desired.

"In fact, ship builders have recognised this. In 1844, the shipbuilder I.K. Brunel, in this quest for the ultimate in passenger comfort, designed the ocean liner *Great Britain*. Its proportions (522 by 51 by 32½ feet) were almost identical to those of the Ark!

"Interestingly, Noah's was the first of its kind – perfect, first hit! – while Brunel had all the accumulated knowledge of shipbuilding expertise upon which to draw. And yet this could *not* give him a ratio more perfect than that of Noah's Ark. After thousands of years of experience, engineers acknowledge these measurements to be perfect.

"Then there was George Dickie, a Scottish architect and a graduate of the University of Edinburgh. He was drawing plans for a ship, when a newspaper article was drawn to his attention. The writer was ridiculing the story of Noah's Ark.

"Dickie consulted the Genesis record. And to his surprise, the Ark's dimensions were similar to those in his own plans. Except for the fact that his dimensions were for a ship just one-seventh smaller than the Ark, the specifications were identical.

"From Dickie's plans, the Union Iron Works of San Francisco constructed the well-known battleship *Oregon*. As a flagship of the U.S. navy, it led convoys, visited almost every notable port of the world and met every test of seaworthiness, including a fierce typhoon.

"Just a moment," I said, fumbling in my bag. "Just take a look at this, Hank."

I pulled out a statement by the editor of the *Los Angeles Times*, referring to the *Oregon*. It said:

"One of the surprising facts of history is that it took 2,000 years for the science of marine engineering to develop the highest type of sea-going craft, when the secrets of the true dimensions for *the greatest carrying power, combined with the least resistance of the waves*, rested all that time in the Book of Genesis."

"Give me that!"

I passed the clipping to Hank.

"I'm stunned!"

"Well, Hank, that ship, the *Oregon*, is a mute witness to any skeptic that the Ark was a scientifically constructed vessel.

"More than that, you have to admit, the wisdom in those measurements lifts the book of Genesis out of the realm of a fanciful tale and into the classification of an up-to-date, reliable account.

"While attending the University of Groningen in the Netherlands, veteran newsman Rene Noorbergen came across a manuscript which mentioned a Dutch merchant by the name of Pieter Jansen. He reports:

" 'In the beginning of the seventeenth century, he commissioned a shipyard to build a scale model of the ark according to the measurements given in the book of Genesis. His scale model is reported to have been 120 feet long, twenty feet wide, and twelve feet high. It proved not only more seaworthy than contemporary vessels, but its gross tonnage was one-third larger than ships built to more modern designs.'[11]

"But it's not just Brunel's, Dickie's or Jansen's ships. Many modern day vessels, from warships to racing sail boats, are built to design specifications similar to those of the Ark."

"Just let me get another drink," announced Hank. He shot off to the kitchen and was back fast. He took a sip and then let me have it.

"Yea, but what about the tidal waves old Noah had to endure? That would have been like nothing we know."

"Okay, let's look at that question. Did you know, Hank, that the eruption of Indonesia's Mount Krakatoa in 1883 created tidal waves 100 feet high on shorelines one-third of the way around the world, but on the ocean they measured only inches in height? That's right. Tidal waves become dangerous only when approaching land mass and are quite survivable in the open sea.

"Really?" Hank scratched his shoulder and got himself more comfortable.   "That's one bit of fascinating stuff, I must admit!"

"But there's more Hank. You see, in any case, the Ark's 515 foot length would ensure that the vessel was not subjected to any wave of equal magnitude acting throughout its entire length. This would lessen the likelihood of capsizing.

"And the cross-section measurement is very significant. For any degree of tilt up to 90 degrees, the Ark would tend to right itself.

"It seems to have been built in the expectation that waves were to roll over the top for most of the time. It was engineered to wallow in the sea like a log. Neither a tidal wave nor a tsunami could not have sunk the Ark.

"So it appears, Hank, that the story of the Ark is both mathematically and hydrodynamically feasible."

NOT EVEN IN SO MIGHTY A TEMPEST AS THE GREAT FLOOD?

Hank opened his mouth... and closed it again.

"Go on," I prodded.

"It was nothing."

"You might as well spit it out."

"Well, I was going to say, perhaps the Ark would have capsized, since it was such a one-of-a-kind Flood, since it was so mighty, sweeping away so much rubble, sweeping away even mountains. Since it was so great, as to stratify the whole planet?"

"Fair question. The answer is, again, that the violence was at the bottom, not at the top of the waters."

CONVINCING THE ANIMALS

"Okay," said Hank with a grin. "Here's another tough one for you. How could Noah have gathered all those animals for the Ark from all over the world? Boy, would he have been busy! Not to mention having to build the Ark at the same time."

"Indeed, you're thorough, old son. But don't people gather animals for zoos today? Of course Noah and his helpers only needed to preserve the basic types, not the whole range of varieties within those types.

"Anyway, I don't think they had to go to the ends of the earth on bring-them-back-alive expeditions.

"Did Noah really have to drive a pair of skunks into a box – trying to manipulate the box, wield a stick and hold his nose, all at the same time?"

"The book of Genesis says other forces were operating. The animals instinctively came to the Ark, perhaps through some intuition of the approaching catastrophe.

"Experts have noted that many animals (both vertebrates and invertebrates) possess the ability to sense imminent danger. They instinctively leave areas due for an earthquake, an eruption or other natural disaster.

"Nevertheless, the co-operation of a *select group* from every species of animal does require something above natural law operating. It requires the natural and supernatural working side by side and hand in hand.

"My friend, all considered, I must suggest this. The combination of events we are talking about - how could they have been anything less than a miracle? If the event occurred, then it seems to me it was masterminded, engineered and controlled from the start. This outside interaction and control by Intelligence did *not* occur by chance."

KANGAROOS, POLAR BEARS, ETC?: TOO FAR TO TRAVEL?

"But," Hank insisted, "surely it would be impossible for animals to come to one single spot from everywhere on earth? I mean, what about the kangaroo in Australia, cut off by a vast ocean? And the polar bear... and the animals from South America?"

"Good one, Hank! Actually, that's not quite as difficult as it may seem. You see, the worldwide uniformity of the pre-Flood climate meant that all types of animals would have been available in special niches all around the globe, and thus available in close proximity to the Ark, as well.

"And there were no vast stretches of water cutting off land areas. If all the mainlands were at one time joined together, as many scientists envisage, travel would have been no problem either.

"Something else, Hank. The human race was given 120 years' probation. So even if not all animals lived nearby, they had adequate time to migrate. In recent times, large migrations of animals over great distances have been known to occur. No problem, the implanted instinct by which the animals migrated to the Ark might have been operative for many generations."

ON-BOARD CARE

"One more question," pressed Hank.

"Fire away."

"What an horrendous task, caring for and feeding so many animals for a whole year in the Ark! What about the feeding of the carnivores? Could even rabbits have bred fast enough to provide adequate sustenance for the tigers?"

"It's virtually certain Hank, they were all young animals. I'm sure that was all worked out ahead of time. They had to survive a year in the Ark, then repopulate the earth. So they would be young. And relatively small and docile.

"In such a time of stress they would feed less and sleep more.

"It is also likely that many, if not most, of the animals spent most of the year in a state of relative dormancy. So they would require a minimum of care. An animal can, by suspending or retarding his natural functions, survive at length during times of dire stress or hardship. Hibernation and estivation occur in every group of vertebrates except birds.[12] And fundamentally, even birds have been seen to possess this latent capacity.

[By the way, on that subject I'll share with you an amazing story. You'll find it in the Appendix.]

"Many scientists admit that this mechanism is still a mystery.

"To cite one authority, Marston Bates, of the Rockefeller Foundation:

" 'Our knowledge of this mechanism is very incomplete, perhaps because it represents a field on the border line between physiology and ecology and is consequently neglected by both sciences. Various theories have been proposed to account for hibernation, and it seems likely that the controlling stimuli may vary with different animals." [13]

"Who knows? Perhaps the lowering of the animals' metabolic rates was accomplished by artificial means, using the scientific knowledge possessed by Noah's family."

"Yeah, that's possible I 'spose, admitted Hank. "And to think I'd considered this whole thing to be a heap of rot. I must admit, it makes quite a bit of sense now."

"Any more questions?"

"No."

"Then do you mind if I ask you a few?"

The guy grinned sheepishly – "Yeah. Let's have it!"

He doubled up another cushion… and looked thoughtful as the questions were counted off…

HOW DID HE KNOW?

These are the questions I asked:

1. *HOW DID NOAH KNOW THE FLOOD WAS COMING – SO MANY YEARS BEFORE?*

No long-term warning has preceded other so-called 'deluges' in history, or, more correctly, locally limited natural catastrophes, whether from the Mount St Helens eruption, or the Tokyo earthquake, or whatever.

Now, the Flood of Noah was a catastrophe beyond our wildest imagination. The watery destruction of this planet's surface was so total that nothing on land could have survived.

My point is this: on this one occasion, if there had been no long term warning, no time to prepare, clearly there could have been no survivors – and you and I would not be here now. The human race could never have survived such a cosmic event WITHOUT some form of protection such as the Ark provided.

What is more, preparation of this floating survival vessel could have been possible only as a result of LONG TERM ADVANCE KNOWLEDGE of the event. Preparation took a lot of time.

So here's my question again: *HOW DID HE KNOW IT WAS COMING, SO MANY DECADES BEFORE THE EVENT?*

It was a once-only event. Such specific forewarning could not have resulted from scientific deduction, since the event was contrary to past experience of the accepted operation of nature.

2. *HOW DID HE KNOW IT WAS TO BE A DISASTER IN WHICH THE PRIME AGENCY WOULD BE WATER?*

The character of the disaster being known 120 years before the event is unprecedented in science. The notion that it may have been a scientific forecast must therefore be rejected.

3. *HOW DID HE KNOW THAT THE SURFACE DESTRUCTION OF THIS PLANET WOULD BE SO COMPLETE THAT THERE WOULD BE NO SURVIVORS?*

This very knowledge is what prompted him to preserve a breeding pair of every life form.

4. *HOW DID HE KNOW WHAT OPTIMUM SPECIFICATIONS TO INCORPORATE IN THE SURVIVAL VESSEL, SO THAT IT WOULD RIDE OUT AN EVENT OF UNPRECEDENTED VIOLENCE?*

   There was no latitude for trial and error. Clearly, with no past experience of such a global cataclysm, the building of the Ark would have been a logistical nightmare.

   Noah had one chance only. And no opportunity for sea trials. Yet he built on land a ship of the best possible dimensions for the greatest carrying power, combined with the least resistance of the waves. Tell me please, *WAS NOAH STABBING IN THE DARK, OR WAS HE GIVEN THE BLUEPRINT, AS GENESIS SAYS?*

5. The precise **boarding time** was likewise important. Take the animals on board too early – whether years, months or weeks too early – and there could be big problems. Or wait until too late… That's too horrible to contemplate.

   "HOW DID NOAH KNOW, AFTER ALL THOSE YEARS OF PREPARATION – HOW DID HE KNOW WHEN THE TIME WAS EXACTLY RIGHT, TO GO ON BOARD?

SUPERNATURAL INTERVENTION?

Hank was deathly silent. I sensed a struggle taking place inside his head. It seemed like hours before he answered.

"If I'm going to be rational about this…"

He faltered. My heart went out to the man. I'd grown to like him. His honesty got to me. And now it was obvious he didn't like what he was about to say.

"Noah… well, to do all those things just right, he couldn't have known by himself. No one could guess things like that. But then… well, he MUST have known. Yes, he knew, didn't he?"

Hank continued in deep thought. "Well, Jonathan, I guess it has to be said… there HAD to be a Superior Intelligence operating in it all. Is that what you call God, or something?"

…Yes, it's simple enough, when you think it through: When you consider the facts in total, one cannot have *any* kind of a Genesis Flood without suspecting the presence of supernatural elements.

There is, after all, compelling evidence that the Great Flood occurred (see Book 2 of this series, *Surprise Witness*). And yet the associated *combination* of factors is - let's face it - beyond natural, every-day explanation.

Doesn't it make you wonder? Could *somebody* have told Noah to prepare – as well as how to prepare? Specific long-term preparation surely demands some kind of knowledge of the future in specific detail.

Genesis states positively, as do the Flood traditions of the whole world, that a favoured family was forewarned. There was sufficient time for fail-proof design and construction of a vessel the size of a modern aircraft carrier.

In such advance provision, the involvement of a Superior Intelligence would appear to be not only likely, but an absolute necessity.

There is nothing in science that conflicts with the concept of a Supreme Intelligence. The question is, could such a One have intervened? An ancient document states "Jehovah sat as King at the Flood."[14]

By its very character the worldwide Flood is one of those special events in history which contain elements beyond purely natural explanation.

NOAH'S ARK – Summary

Many people reject the Bible story of Noah's Flood simply because the Ark is pictured as a tiny vessel sitting helpless before the slightest squall.

CAPACITY   The question arises, Is it not absurd to think that all the species of animals on earth could have fitted into one little boat?

But was it so small? The account states that the Ark was of three decks and was 300 cubits (515 feet) long. With the capacity of a freight train three miles long, it would have displaced some 32,000 or more tons. Using only 41 percent of available space, representatives of all mammals, reptiles and birds could have fitted aboard the Ark. The real question is, What did Noah do with all that extra room?

"But," the objection is raised, "vessels of such size could not have been constructed in ancient times."

Such a question arises from ignorance of our past. Actually, the further back we go, the more sophisticated does shipbuilding technology appear to be. Civilisations later entered into decline and the memory of them was forgotten. Antedeluvian technology was quite able to produce a vessel of the dimensions claimed for the Ark.

PROPORTIONS AND STABILITY   From the standpoint of seaworthiness in a storm, engineers acknowledge the measurements of the Ark to be perfect. Many modern vessels are built to design specifications similar to those of the Ark. Optimum design has been achieved only from long experience, often after fatal errors. The scientific wisdom displayed in the Ark's construction lift this ancient story out of the realm of fanciful tale and into the classification of an up-to-date, reliable account.

THE ANIMALS Known natural mechanisms could well have operated in the migration of the animals to the Ark, their willingness to mingle and their hibernation aboard during the Flood duration. In the light of modern scientific knowledge, these aspects no longer present a problem.

SUPERNATURAL INTERVENTION   Advance knowledge of the event, which enabled preparation of a survival vessel and the preservation of representative animal life suggests that the occasion was engineered, controlled and masterminded from the start.   The combination of events is beyond natural explanation.   It suggests a Higher Intelligence at work.

14

Ages in chaos -

DATING SHOCK

Get ready for a SHOCK! Perhaps even anger. Some powerful men are trying to keep us in the dark. These same men control what our children learn. Let me explain.

SOME HOT QUESTIONS

To fulfil its stated purpose, the Deluge had to be a total wipe-out. It was a re-structuring event, which altered every square foot of the planet's surface. Furthermore, this occurred "only" 4 to 5,000 years ago.

If, indeed, this is true history, then the popularised geological time-table is wrong. It also means that all of us have descended in very recent times from the sons of Noah.

Now, I realise this will raise further questions, such as these:

1. What about carbon dating?
2. What about the Australian Aborigines? Haven't they lived undisturbed for 20,000, 40,000, even 60,000 years? So what does this do to a WORLDWIDE Flood of 2345 B.C?
3. How could all the variations in the human race have occurred in just a few thousand years since the time of Noah?

Hot questions. And important. Our awareness of who we are – and where we're going – is at stake.

By the way, I noticed a news item the other day, which said that some Aboriginal cave paintings had been found, that were 30,000 years old.

Frankly, I should be envious. If I buy a can of Bergers paint and use it to paint my house, it lasts 20 to 30 years. Yet here's some Aborigine who has got some ochre and blows it on a cave wall with a blowpipe – and it has lasted 30,000 years?

Where can I get a can of that stuff?

145

We shall, in these final three chapters, consider these fascinating questions concerning how old things really are. Are you ready?

TWO OPPOSING SYSTEMS

According to the genealogy lists in the Bible, the Creation of life on this earth was not much more than 6,000 years ago.

The dominant popular theory today demands that life on earth is at least 4½ billion years old. And the earth's physical features do look old, don't they?

Obviously, between these two extremes of thinking there is a very great gulf. One of them is ridiculously wrong!

RADIOMETRIC DATING

The methods that can give us ideas of the earth's age ("geological clocks", one calls them) are all based on the knowledge that natural processes which occur steadily through time will produce cumulative and often measurable results.

Three popular dating methods are uranium into lead, potassium into argon, and rubidium into strontium. In each case, when a molten rock cools and solidifies, then any radio-active "parent" element is supposed to decay into its "daughter" element at a known, slow rate. The amount of each in a rock will tell us the "age" of that rock.

I'll go along with that. Sounds like it should be easy to prove the age of the earth.

ASSUMPTIONS

Of course, in dealing with a specimen, there are several things we must first assume:
1.   That the *rate* of decay is constant;
2.   That none of the daughter element was already present when the rock solidified;
3.   That no parent or daughter elements were added *or* leached out of the rock over the years.

It's a pity, but these assumptions MUST be made. And as much as we might wish it otherwise, this initial stage cannot be science. It is merely a reasoned opinion about the specimen in hand. One must reason that there is nothing we have to worry about that could have happened in the past.

Oh to know for sure! Unfortunately, we cannot.

1. Assumed *constant rate of decay*:
    There is now evidence that the rate of decay *can change* as the pressure changes. [1] And other factors can alter it.
    As Frederic B. Jueneman laments:
    "The age of our globe is presently thought to be some 4.5 billion years, based on radiodecay rates of uranium and thorium. Such 'confirmation' may be short-lived, as nature is not to be discovered quite so easily. There has been in recent years the horrible realization that radiodecay rates are not as constant as previously thought, nor are they immune to environmental influences.
    "And this could mean that the atomic clocks are reset during some global disaster, and events which brought the Mesozoic to a close may not be 65 million years ago but, rather, within the age and memory of man." [2]

2. Assumed *ratio of parent to daughter element(s)* in the rock sample:
    Henry Faul, editor of *Nuclear Geology*, acknowledges that in a uranium mineral, the lead ("daughter") can be both derived from disintegrating uranium AND ORIGINAL. [3]
    Radiogenic lead has been found in uranium minerals even in *recently formed* volcanic rock.

3. Assumption that there has been *no adding or leaching out of the rock* of these elements:
    It is, unfortunately, impossible to know this. For example, potassium (used for dating) can be easily leached out of rock by rainwater percolating through it. Argon, produced by the decay of potassium, can easily diffuse through rock. And pressure will affect the rate of diffusion.
    Nobel Prize medallist Melvin Cook has found that lead may change its isotopic value by the capture of free neutrons from the environment and that the age of such uranium-bearing rocks containing lead may be essentially zero! [4]
    Geologists Klepper and Wyant declare:
    "Most igneous rocks also contain uranium in a form that is readily soluble in weak acids. Hurley (1950) found that as much as 90 percent of the total radioactive elements of some granites

could be removed by leaching the granulated rock with weak acid... Larsen and Phair (in Faul, 1954, p.80) note that 'commonly, as much as 40 percent of the uranium in most fresh-appearing igneous rocks is readily leachable'." [5]

The fact that these unstable, soluble minerals in the rocks cannot withstand erosion and leaching even for a few years, renders them useless as time clocks.

Just a moment! Something's wrong here!

CARBON DATING

Well, perhaps carbon dating is more reliable.

Carbon dating is used to determine how long ago something died.

It is based on the radioactive decay rate in organic matter. It is a known fact that every living thing absorbs cosmic radio-active carbon-14 from the atmosphere. At death, this intake ceases and the radiocarbon in the organism begins to disintegrate. The amount of remaining C-14 is used to calculate how long ago the organism died.

The validity of carbon dating depends on three assumptions:

1. That the amount of cosmic radiation in the atmosphere has remained constant at all times in all places;
2. That the sample tested has not been contaminated by recent microbes or bacteria;
3. That there has been no exchange with the outside world.

When carbon dating was first announced by Dr. Libby in 1949, it was thought to be the last word, but that early confidence is no longer justified.

It has been discovered that cosmic radiations vary widely, due to many factors, natural and industrial.

Suppose you enter a sealed room which contains nothing but a burning candle. You are asked to determine how long the candle has been burning.

Picture: Dennis R. Petersen

You soon realise how impossible this is. You could measure the relative amounts of oxygen and carbon dioxide in the room; or you could try to figure out how long the melted wax took to accumulate.

But you cannot know whether someone had opened and re-shut the window. Was it ever put out and re-lit? Could some interruption have caused it to burn faster?

There is room for enormous error.

Dating cannot deal with unique events. They're gone. You cannot re-run them. You cannot repeat a test on them.

Every dating method we operate today is invalid as a scientific test for the past. You cannot guarantee it. It remains nothing more than a reasoned guess.

There are so many unknown factors to consider. And these are not appreciated by many scientists who use the method itself.

Science cannot deal with the past. Consequently, there is no test available now that can give you a scientifically guaranteed date for the past. All we can do is use the methods about which we can make assumptions that are reasonable.

So when you're told a certain date has been proved, you're hearing someone who either doesn't understand the scientific test, or who (hopefully not) is lying to you.

SOMETIMES DATES OBTAINED FROM 2 OR MORE RADIOMETRIC METHODS AGREE. DOESN'T THIS PROVE THE ACCURACY OF RADIOMETRIC DATING?

In view of the *rarity* of such agreements, it may well be that such are fortuitous coincidences.

149

Be clear on this: there is no large body of concordant data, but there is a massive body of discordant data.

As one authority admits:

"Age estimates on a given geological stratum by different radiometric methods are often quite different (sometimes by hundreds of millions of years). There is no absolutely reliable long-term radiological 'clock'. The uncertainties inherent in radiometric dating are disturbing to geologists and evolutionists." [6]

When dating recent creatures and artefacts, radiometric dating methods have been known to be accurate in certain cases. But don't bet your life on it.

UNRELIABILITY EXAMPLES

- Living mollusc shells showed ages of 1,010 to 2,300 years, as though they had been dead for that time! [7]
- The "apparent radiocarbon age of a Lake Bonney seal known to have been dead no more than a few weeks was determined to be 615± 100 years. A seal freshly killed at McMurdo had an apparent age of 1,300 years." [8]
- Carbon-14 tests on some snails which were still alive showed that they 'died' 27,000 years ago. [9]
- A critical analysis of the available lead data shows ages obtained which extend millions of years into the future! [10] According to isotopic ratios for common lead found in rocks, many of our rocks should not exist, but will only come into being far into the future. [11] Geologists discard such date results. Perhaps it is the method that should be discarded?
- In 1966, a hand-crafted tool made of caribou bone (found in the Yukon, Canada) was carbon dated at 25,000 to 32,000 years. However, in 1986, tissues of the bone were protein-tested and the date obtained was just over 2,000 years of age. [12]
- The same piece of basalt rock from Nigeria gave ages (by different methods) from 2 to 750 million years. [13]
- In eight separate tests, scientists dated samples of rock – and arrived at ages of 160 million to 3 billion years. These specimens, from Kaupelehu, Hualalai Volcano, Hawaii,

were later found to have formed in a lava flow only 168 years earlier, in 1801. [14]

- A skeleton from California was estimated at 70,000 years old (by a technique called a partic acid racemization). [15] In 1981 this age was revised to 8,300 to 9,000 years (by uranium dating). [16] In 1983 samples of the same skeleton were dated at 3,500 to 5,000 years (by radiocarbon dating).[17]

- Muscle tissue from beneath the scalp of a mummified musk ox in Fairbanks Creek, Alaska, was dated at 24,000 years; hair from a hind limb of the same animal was dated at 7,200 years. Poor creature. What a long, slow death it must have suffered!

- Human remains found deep in the delta deposit near New Orleans, Louisiana, were dated at 57,000 years – but when wood from the gunwhale of a Kentucky flatboat was found deeper, the 57,000 years shrank to 200 or less.

- Pottery in the Nile mud was publicised to be 30,000 years old – until it was proved to be a piece of Roman pottery of recent date.

- In New Zealand, volcanic material with "ages" ranging from 145,000 to 465,000 years overlies destroyed trees with a radiocarbon age of only 225 years.

- On June 30, 1908, a colossal and mysterious explosion took place at Tunguska, in Siberia. Objects at the epicentre of the explosion have been carbon dated. Nicola Jones, writing in *New Scientist*, noted but otherwise avoided the fact that the concentration of carbon 14 at the epicentre is so high that radiometric dating places the Tunguska Event in the future! [18]

Oh, how fascinating! And countless more examples could be given. Something is wrong – drastically wrong. This kind of evidence should be enough to discredit the system.

It suggests that our dating systems may be in error... but we can't have that!

DISCORDANT DATES NOT PUBLICISED

Most published dates are from discordant data. More significantly, most discordant data are never published at all.

So what dates get published in reputable scientific journals?

Notice. And it's Richard L. Mauger, Associate Professor of Geology, East Carolina, speaking:

"In general, dates in the 'correct ball park' are assumed to be correct and are published, but those in disagreement with other data are seldom published nor are discrepancies fully explained."[19]

Whatever the figures arrived at by the dating tests, they are weeded out before publication in scientific journals, if they do not accord with the pre-conceived dates assigned to the evolutionary geological column.[20]

That's a fact. But don't get upset with *me.* It's some of the men involved who are admitting it.

DINOSAUR DATING

Scientists at Oak Ridge National Laboratories in the U.S.A. used uranium dating on wood in rocks of a dinosaur stratum – and they obtained ages of only *thousands* of years.

We don't hear about such things, do we?

As for the carbon-14 theory, it has drawn so much criticism in recent years that few archaeologists accept its results, and never accept the C-14 "age" when it contradicts historical dates.

WHY DO SCIENTISTS STILL
USE SUCH DATING?

Robert E. Lee writes:

"The implications of pervasive contamination and ancient variations in carbon-14 levels are steadfastly ignored by those who base their argument upon the dates... Surely 15,000 years of difference on a single block of soil is indeed a *gross* discrepancy! And how could the excessive disagreement between the labs be called insignificant, when it has been the basis for the reappraisal of the standard error associated with each and every date in existence?

"Why do geologists and archaeologists still spend their scarce money on costly radiocarbon determinations? They do so because occasional dates *appear* to be useful. While the method cannot be counted on to give good, unequivocal results, the numbers do impress people, and save them the trouble of thinking excessively. Expressed in what *look* like precise calendar years, figures *seem* somehow better... 'Absolute' dates determined by a laboratory carry a lot of weight, and are extremely helpful in bolstering weak arguments.'...

"... the accepted dates are actually *selected* dates. "This whole blessed thing is nothing but 13th-century alchemy, and it all depends upon which funny paper you read.' " [21] It should be noted that this man speaks as an evolutionist.

MOST DATE READINGS ARE DISCARDED

Another authority concedes:

"If a C14 date supports our theories, we put it in the main text. If it does not entirely contradict them, we put it in a footnote. And if it is completely 'out of date', we just drop it." [22]

Let it be stressed that discordant results are the rule and not the exception.

AN HONEST ADMISSION

Although some scientists using carbon-14 dating will propose dates extending back 50,000 years and even further, Dr. George Howe acknowledges that "the men who know the limits of the method, the men who run the tests, would report that they cannot date with accuracy beyond 3,000 years." [23]

He states that Geochron Laboratories will return samples to clients if they give a date above 3,000 years, with comments that they are above the age that can be accurately dated.

WHY ARE "OLD" DATES SOUGHT?

Most people are not aware that the very existence of long geological ages is based on the assumption of evolution. A magic wand is needed to make it "work". That magic wand is "billions of years".

If the earth is only thousands of years old, then there is obviously no time for the slow evolutionary process to have occurred. The alternative, Creation, makes many people quite uncomfortable.

So to say that human remains at least a million years old have been found, has become a habit.

The truth is, the average anthropologist has no more knowledge of the actual date than the street pedlar.

MOST "CLOCKS" GIVE A YOUNG AGE

Remember. Dating methods do NOT prove the earth to be old.

In an original paper in *Science*, Patterson, Tilton and Ingham advised great CAUTION in accepting the actuality of the dating of 4.5 billion years. In fact, they were quite skeptical. [24]

Dr. D. Russell Humphreys, a physicist working for the prestigious Sandia National Laboratories in Albuquerque, New Mexico, and a winner of several scientific awards, makes this illuminating comment:

"I estimate that there are probably several hundred processes that one could use to get an idea of the age of the earth. Only a few dozen, at most, of these processes seem to give you billions of years. The other 90 percent of those processes give you ages much less than billions of years. So it seems like it would be good science to go with the flow of the 90 percent of the data, and use as a working hypothesis that the earth really is young and then try to find explanations for the other 10 percent of the data.

"That whole process seems to be a much more scientific approach than the one that is taken by evolutionists. Basically, they concentrate on the 10 percent of the data, and that's the data you've always heard about." [25]

Totally different methods give consistent indications that the earth is less than 20,000 years old.

Only a few of the "clocks" yield a conclusion of billions of years. These few are LOUDLY PUBLICISED to support the popular theory of uniformism (for evolution).

This information is scientifically known – but generally not publicised.

It is time to ask:

WHY IS THIS HIDDEN FROM THE GENERAL PUBLIC?

A cover-up is in full swing. I'll tell you about that next.

15

How old is the earth, really? -

THE COVER-UP

We come now to the most astounding unpublicised fact with respect to dating by the carbon-14 system.

This technique has, during its development, uncovered some startling, though publicly undisclosed, evidence of an earth less than 10,000 years old.

Here it is. Through the action of solar rays, radio-active carbon is being formed in the atmosphere at a constant rate. This carbon-14 ultimately enters all living tissues; and much more is absorbed into the ocean. From the time of its formation, it begins a slow decay.

Theoretically, the amount decaying per day *should be equal to* the amount being produced by cosmic rays in the upper atmosphere. The success of carbon-14 dating depends on this equilibrium.

Here is a vital question. How long would it take for the carbon-14 on earth to build up from almost zero to equilibrium?

Scientists have calculated that *from the time the build-up began* (in the atmosphere, seas and living tissues), it would take about 30,000 years to reach the volume where daily decay equalled the amount being produced.

STILL BUILDING UP

Does such equilibrium exist? NOT AT ALL!

Balloon soundings show that much more C-14 is still being formed than is decaying. Nobel Prize medallist Dr. Melvin Cook, using data from several tests, has determined that the carbon-14 content of our atmosphere *is STILL BUILDING UP! This could be so only if the process had begun recently.* The production-decay rates are out of equilibrium by as much as 38 percent! [1]

Dr. Cook calculates that such discrepancy between formation and decay indicates an age for our atmosphere of no more than 10,000 years. The likelihood that C-14 was produced at a rate up to three times greater in the past (as evidenced by luxuriant flora and fauna in the worldwide fossil record), would reduce this figure to a mere 6- to 7,000 years.

Thus all carbon-14 dates, when corrected for the known non-equilibrium conditions, would show less than 7,000 years.

W.F. Libby, the discoverer of the C-14 technique, chose to ignore the discrepancy, attributing it to some error of measurement, since he "knew" the earth to be much older than 30,000 years.

Subsequent and better tests have confirmed this lack of equilibrium.

However, this is routinely rejected. The evolutionary theory, which has permeated the thinking of most scientists, demands great ages. Consequently such data is not discussed in PUBLIC literature.

SPEED OF LIGHT OVERTURNS DATING

The atomic clock measures time by the speed of radioactive decay. And this has given ages of billions of years for the earth.

However, in 1987, two independent research reports - the first from Stanford Research Institute, the second by a Soviet physicist - demonstrated that the atomic clock is affected by the behavior of the speed of light. And the speed of light has slowed dramatically. [2]

According to the Stanford study, light originally travelled about 11 million times its current speed. The second study placed it at roughly 10 billion times faster than now. Radioactive decay was, therefore, faster to the same magnitude.

A correction, once made, brings radiometric dating into closer alignment with biblical dating.

Nothing in science disproves the biblical claim that our earth is only THOUSANDS of years old and that every earth feature was RESHAPED by the Deluge about 2345 B.C. This also reset some of our dating clocks.

SOME OF THE "YOUNG" CLOCKS
The moon is receding:

The moon's distance from the earth is increasing at 2 inches a year. Working back, this would mean that the moon and earth would be touching 2 billion years ago. Or, looking at it another way, at the present rate, and starting at a realistic distance of separation, if the earth is 5 billion years old, the moon should be out of sight by now!

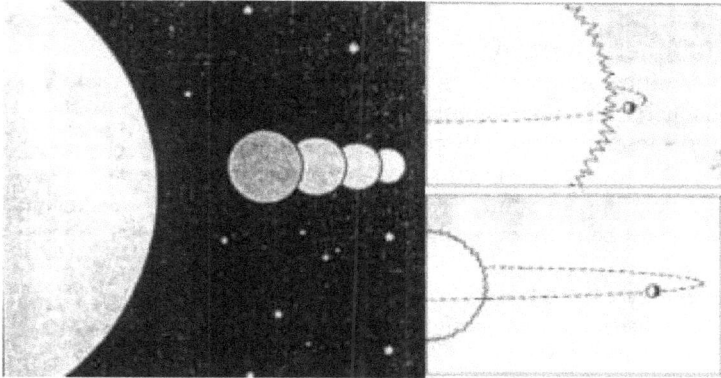

Drawings: Dennis R. Petersen

The sun is shrinking:

The sun's diameter is shrinking one tenth percent per century, or every hour about 5 feet (1.5 metres).

If the sun existed only 20 million years ago, the surface of the sun would be touching the earth.

Perhaps the sun and earth just aren't that old!

Salt influx into the ocean:

Salt is being continually washed into the sea. At the present rates of accumulation (and assuming there was no salt there in the first place, assuming also that no salt is being precipitated out of the ocean, and allowing also for the formation of rock salt by evaporation, and that the rate of inflow has always been the same), it would take an absolute maximum of 260 million years for the various elements to accumulate in the ocean from river inflow.

This is far short of the 1,000 million years required by evolution. Life began in the sea? The sea is not old enough – if we use the evolutionist's own method, uniformitarianism – to determine its age.

However, since the waters of the Great Flood flushed out the various elements rapidly from the continental soils, before retreating to the oceans, we could not be talking in millions of years at all. The present river inflow is minimal compared to what occurred during the Great Flood and its immediate aftermath.

Atmospheric helium:

Helium is steadily gathering in the outer reaches of our atmosphere. The total amount there can be measured.

If the earth were billions of years old, the atmosphere would be saturated with a million times more helium than exists now.

According to some experts, the helium "clock" insists that the earth cannot be more than 10,000 to 15,000 years old.

The decay of magnetism

Scientists have brought to light the fact that the earth's magnetism is decaying.

Dr. Thomas G. Barnes, Professor of Physics at the University of Texas, El Paso, and a consultant to Globe Universal Sciences, Inc., points out that our earth's magnetic field has a half-life, or loses half its strength, every 1,400 years. This means that 1,400 years ago the magnetic field was twice as strong as now, and so on.

The earth's magnetic moment is at present only 37 percent as strong as it was in the days of Jesus Christ. From the magnetic field an electric current flows through the core of the earth. It uses energy and produces heat. The present energy loss is 8.13 million watts.

Says Dr. Maurice Dametz, "The rate of decay is so rapid that the earth cannot be more than 15,000 years old." [3]

EARTH FEATURES FORMED RAPIDLY

Did you know that such features as

SANDY BEACHES, RAISED BEACHES, CAVES, COVES, ETC.,

do not need a long time to form?

In 1963, the new island of Surtsey appeared 70 km south of Iceland.

The following year a landing party found wide, sandy beaches, precipitous crags, gravel banks, lagoons, impressive cliffs resembling England's White Cliffs, faulted cliffs and boulders worn smooth by the surf, some of which were round. [4]

BUT WHAT ABOUT:
- Stalactites?

Far from requiring vast aeons, stalactites can grow quite rapidly, given sufficient mineral-laden water.

For centuries after the Flood, caves received greater seepage of lime-bearing water than now. In those wetter times, deposits formed very rapidly.

In the basement of the Shrine of Remembrance in Melbourne, Australia, large stalactites were found to have grown in only 59 years. One was sent to Monash University and another to the National University in Canberra. They came back with declared ages of from 120,000 years minimum to 300,000 years maximum. When this dating was challenged, a university response was: "But they HAVE TO be that old!"

The massive vaults beneath the shrine resemble the interior of limestone caves, with thousands of stalactites and stalagmites. In fact, stalactites have been found growing under many modern buildings. So whenever you see one hanging from a building, try to figure out how many thousands of years old you think that building is!

159

Photo: Craig Borrow and the Herald and Weekly Times

- Fossil coral reefs?

Are fossil coral reefs proof of long aeons of time? No. And they're different from modern reefs.

"Closer inspection of many of these ancient carbonate 'reefs' reveals that they are composed largely of carbonate mud with the larger skeletal particles 'floating' within the mud matrix. Conclusive evidence for a rigid framework does not exist in most of the ancient carbonate mounds." [5]

For example, the El Capitan Permian "reef complex" in West Texas is *not a true reef at all*, but largely an "allochthonous", that is, a deposit of fossil-bearing lithified lime transported into place from elsewhere.

- Oil pressure?

Oil (formed by fossilised animal matter) and coal (vegetable matter) are said to be millions of years old. But are they?

Quite frequently, abnormally high pressures of up to 8,000 psi are encountered in deep oil wells. Often when a new well is tapped, a gusher goes spouting into the air due to the tremendous pressure trapped below.

According to measured values of the permeability of surrounding rock, such pressures would dissipate in thousands, not millions of years.

If those oil deposits had been there for more than 5,000 years in some cases there would be no pressure left! Since the pressure is still there (often seeping at the surface), the rock formations containing the oil must be "young".

- Antarctic ice?

That apparently magic expression "million years" is likewise applied to the Antarctic ice cap.

Now 14,000 feet above sea level, the ice continues to build up. In 1930, Admiral Byrd established a base in Antarctica.

Since that time, the ice has piled higher, so that of his 110 foot radio towers, just a few feet now protrude above the icy surface.

At that rate, the ice cover is only 7,000 years old, not a million. But since the build-up must have been more rapid during the Ice Age, it is probably very much younger even than 7,000 years.

But what about the annual ice rings? Don't they prove long ages? No. These are not NOT rings made annually, but daily, by the alternating warmer day and colder night temperatures. I shall discuss this in the third book of this series.

- Canyons?

Many of us were taught in school that when you see a canyon with a river running through it, you assume that the river took a long time to erode the canyon.

How easy it is to come to wrong conclusions if you were not present to see an event, and if you don't have access to all information!

When Mount St. Helens erupted in 1980, some associated events accomplished in days, geological work that would normally be interpreted as having taken millions of years.

Little Grand Canyon (about a one-fortieth scale model of the Grand Canyon) is around 100 feet deep and somewhat wider. Little Grand Canyon was formed *IN ONE DAY* from a mud-flow that eroded material which had been blocking the North Fork of the Toutle Riber.

The new river subsequently flowed through the canyon formed by the mud flow.

Engineers' Canyon, 200 feet wide, was formed, with a tiny stream flowing through it. The stream did *not* slowly form the canyon; this canyon formed the stream.

Engineers Canyon formed very rapidly after the Mount St. Helens eruption –
It did not take long ages. Photo: Steve Austin

At Loowit Canyon, mud blasted through hard rock to cut the canyon in a short time. Perhaps we should realise that engineers have a tool used to cut steel, which basically uses water under pressure. Here, in this blast zone of the volcanic eruption, water, mud and steam, under pressure, produced results in a very short time that evolutionists are telling the world would take millions of years.

In Little Grand Canyon, a hurricane velocity wind of 100 miles per hour (160 kilometres per hour) laid down in just *one day* a *minutely layered strata deposit.* This 25-feet-thick deposit consisted of THOUSANDS of thin strata (layers) – layer upon layer of material, formed by flowing 'rivers' of volcanic ASH. Think! Did the Grand Canyon strata really need millions of years to form?

- magnetic reversals?
PROBLEM: When lava cools down, it freezes into itself information about the direction and strength of the earth's magnetic field at the time. The earth's rocks have frozen into them the record of

MANY REVERSALS of the earth's field – in which the earth's polarity has changed from north to south and back again.

It is generally believed that such reversals could not take place in less than hundreds of thousands, or even millions of years.

ANSWER: There are on earth countless local magnetic fields that can strongly influence and affect measurements in any given locality.

But there is something else. Surprising new data on this subject appeared in *Earth and Planetary Science Letters*.

In 1989, Robert S. Coe and Michael Prevot reported finding a thin lava layer which had 90 degrees of reversal recorded continuously in it. They calculated that the layer had to cool down within a matter of 15 days or less. (It was probably more like only 3 to 7 days.)

This was very surprising to them. Their paper is filled with statements like "astonishingly fast change in the earth's magnetic field" and "truly strains the imagination".[6]

Since then Coe has found similar data which indicates an even faster change than the one first reported. It was in a different rock stratum.

Coe commented that others in his field "don't want to believe it".[7] But he and Prevot had checked their results in several different ways and covered all angles. So the response of other scientists in the same field was one of cautious acceptance. There was a cautious review in *Nature* which accepted their work, but rather reluctantly.

However, there is something else you should know. You see, it has been claimed that the Mid-Atlantic Ridge shows evidence of such long term reversals. But this is clearly a mistake.

The truth is that on the bottom of the ocean along the Mid-Atlantic Ridge were found areas of stronger and weaker magnetism – not reversals.

As an instrument was dragged across the area, the signals showed a wave pattern of stronger – weaker – stronger – weaker, and so on.

The conclusion was: "It is clear that the simple model of uniformly magnetized crustal blocks of alternating polarity **does not represent reality**." [8]

Magnetic reversals in the Mid-Atlantic Ridge? NO! Nice neat lines of **alternating polarity? No!** There are no magnetic reversals on the ocean floor. There are **only areas of weaker magnetism.**

What happened during the Flood was this: Water burst up through the basalt, which cracked open a great rift. The land both sides slid away a little and the basalt rose in the middle. The rising caused a series of parallel cracks. Water entering the cracks cooled and solidified the basalt layer into a stronger magnetic field.

You see, basalt, if it is hot, does not store a stronger magnetic signature, whereas if it is cooled off it stores a stronger magnetic signature.

So all they were measuring is where the cracks are in the Mid-Atlantic Ridge – with alternating stronger and weaker magnetism. There's no magnetic reversal. There is no place where a north-seeking compass will point north, then south, by the rocks down there.

Scientists have not been reckoning with a cosmic catastrophe like the Great Flood and what it might do to the earth's core. So this remains an enigma to them.

ONE OTHER THING: DNA IN FOSSILS

Fossils are supposed to be millions of years old, if the evolution theory is valid.

Complicated long-chain chemicals like DNA and protein tend to break down into simpler pieces by themselves, over time. DNA, the complex molecule of heredity, breaks down, by itself, at an observed, measurable rate.

To preserve DNA over centuries would require special conditions free from moisture and excluding bacteria.

Brian Sykes, in *Nature*, clearly states that the rate at which DNA breaks down in the laboratory is such that after 10,000 years no DNA should be left.[9]

But DNA has now been discovered in magnolia leaf fossils (and oak, cypress and tulip tree fossils) which are in rock layers supposed to be around 20 million years old.

Two separate teams of U.S. researchers have extracted DNA sequences from a termite and a stingless bee. These creatures were so perfectly preserved that even the cell structure could be seen. They were trapped in amber (fossilised tree resin), of evolutionary age 30 million years.[10]

However, the discovery of DNA indicates that they are not 30 million, but less than 10,000 years old.

PROTEIN STILL IN DINOSAURS

More surprises! Dinosaur bones have yielded the protein osteocalcin. Since long chains such as proteins also naturally fall apart, such a discovery supports a "recent" age for these fossils.[11]

In 1961, a petroleum geologist discovered a large bone bed in northwestern Alaska. Among these were bones of duckbill dinosaurs, horned dinosaurs and large and small carnivorous dinosaurs. At the time of writing, William A. Clemens and other scientists from the University of California and Berkeley and the University of Alaska were quarrying the bone bed.[12]

Now, here is the problem: these bones are still in **fresh condition**. They are not fossilised. And they were **not preserved by cold**. It is standard geological interpretation that even **after the dinosaurs died out**, the entire planet was **much warmer**.

Dr. Margaret Helder, science editor of *Reformed Perspective* magazine, comments on this find:

"These recent developments are certainly food for thought. It is undeniable that fresh dinosaur bones have been found. Items have appeared in the secular literature saying exactly that. It is also evident that preservation in the fresh state for even one million years is highly unlikely.

"The obvious conclusion is that these bones were deposited in relatively recent times. This bone bed is stunning evidence that the time of the dinosaurs was not millions of years ago, but perhaps only thousands. It is time geologists recognised the implications of their own data."[13]

UNFOSSILISED BLOOD CELLS
FOUND IN DINOSAUR BONES

Real blood cells in dinosaur bones? With traces of the blood protein hemoglobin?

Preposterous!... that is, if you think these dinosaur remains are 65 million years old or more.

Okay, let me share with you the discovery.

In the United States in 1990, the bones of a beautifully preserved *Tyrannosaurus Rex* skeleton were unearthed. When these were brought to the Montana State University's laboratory, it was noticed that "some parts deep inside the long bone of the leg had not completely fossilized."[14]

Mary Schweitzer and her co-workers took turns looking through a microscope at a thin section of this dinosaur bone, complete with blood vessel channels.

She says: "The lab filled with murmurs of amazement, for I had focused on something inside the vessels that none of us had ever noticed before: tiny round objects, translucent red with a dark center. Then a colleague took one look at them and shouted, "You've got red blood cells. You've got red blood cells!"

Schweitzer says, "I got goose bumps. It was exactly like looking at a slice of modern bone."

She confronted her boss, famous paleontologist 'Dinosaur' Jack Horner.

"I can't believe it," she said. "The bones, after all, are 65 million years old. How could blood cells survive that long?"

"How about you try to prove they are NOT red blood cells," responded Horner.

So she tried. And the verdict? "So far, we haven't been able to." The evidence that hemoglobin (the protein which makes blood red and carries oxygen) has indeed survived in this dinosaur bone casts immense doubt upon the 'millions of years' idea. Here is that evidence:

- The tissue was colored reddish brown, the color of hemoglobin, as was liquid extracted from the dinosaur tissue.
- Hemoglobin contains heme units. Chemical signatures unique to heme were found in the specimens when certain wavelengths of laser light were applied.
- Because it contains iron, heme reacts to magnetic fields differently from other proteins - extracts from this specimen reacted in the same way as modern heme compounds.

- To ensure that the samples had not been contaminated with certain bacteria which have heme (but never the protein hemoglobin), extracts of the dinosaur fossil were injected over several weeks into rats. If there was even a minute amount of hemoglobin present in the *Tyrannosaurus Rex* sample, the rats' immune system should build up detectable antibodies against this compound. This is exactly what happened in carefully controlled experiments.

Evidence of hemoglobin, and the still-recognizable shapes of red blood cells in unfossilized dinosaur bone, testifies strongly that this dinosaur did not live and die millions of years ago. The process of biochemical decay starts soon after death. These cells should long since have disintegrated... unless they are just a few thousand years old.

It hasn't been so long!

* * * * * * *

A DESPISED OLD BOOK IS THE WINNER

Clearly those "crazy" Bible dates are not as suspect as seemed possible 40 years ago. They have stood investigation far better than the very systems of dating which some claimed would outdate Bible chronology.

A TREMENDOUS ERROR

Orthodox science has made an enormous error of interpretation. This cannot remain permanently ignored or suppressed from the public, no matter how defensive the long-date theorists may feel. If it's about our origins, there can be no shadow of a cover up. The public who support them with taxes deserve better than that.

* * * * * * *

All very well, Jonathan, someone says. So tell me, what about the human race and all its variations? If the world was wiped out, except for a single group of survivors, then how on earth could all today's variations and skin colors have developed in just a few thousand years since that event?

You've raised an interesting question.

So let's see...

16

Have all races appeared since Noah?

NOT ENOUGH TIME?

The hands and face of Jaron Yaltan are a pallid white – like those of millions of other Englishmen.

Only the edges of his ears are different, if you look closely. They are brown.

This is the sole clue – outwardly – to the fact that Jaron Yaltan is a white man who was born black in Ahmedabad, South India.

In 1982, when he was 60, the brown fell away in huge patches as the rare pigment cell disorder vitiligo changed his colour within the space of six days.

It has aroused radical reaction from his former friends.

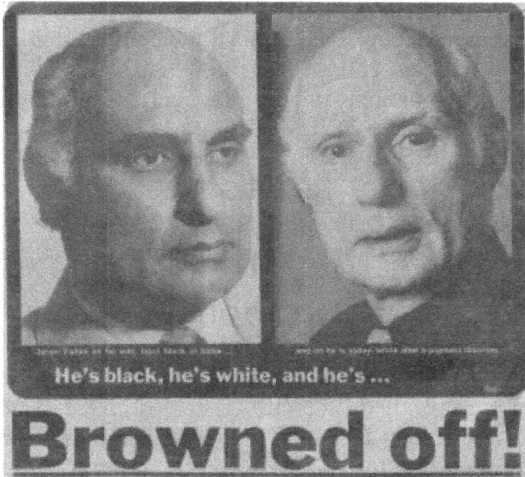

He's black, he's white, and he's ...

Browned off!

"This is the white man's burden. I am carrying it now," says Jaron. "And, believe me, it is very heavy."

This brings us to a fascinating question:

IF THE WORLD WAS WIPED OUT, EXCEPT FOR A SINGLE GROUP OF SURVIVORS, THEN HOWEVER COULD ALL TODAY'S VARIATIONS IN THE HUMAN RACE HAVE OCCURRED IN JUST A FEW THOUSAND YEARS SINCE THAT TIME?

What about the Australian Aborigines, for example, and the Chinese, and so on?

Frankly, I'll confess that for ages I found this to be a problem for scientific

acceptance of a 100 percent Great Flood total wipe-out.

That's because I did not know enough about genetics.

Take *skin colour*, for example. If you didn't know, mankind actually has only one skin colour. That colour shows up as different shades in proportion to the *amount of melanin* in the skin. (Melanin is a colouring compound.)

Melanin protects our bodies by absorbing ultra-violet (UV) radiation from sunlight which falls on the skin.

Darker-skinned people have more melanin, which renders their skin more sunlight resistant. Thus they are better suited to hotter climates. Lighter-skinned people are better suited to a cooler environment.

GOVERNED BY TWO PAIRS OF GENES

Research has shown that there are 19 alleles for skin color, but for the sake of simplicity, let us suppose right now that there are only two genes.

John Mckay B.Sc. writes that "if a person from a pure white European background marries a person from a pure black Negro background, their children will be an intermediate brown colour. This brownish colour is called 'mulatto'. If two MULATTOS marry, unlike their parents they DO NOT produce children which have the same colour. The offspring can be ANY OF NINE COLOURS, from pure white through to pure black."

Thus "if we started today with one pair of middle-brown coloured people (similar to the mulattos), we could produce all the racial colours in the world, NOT IN MILLIONS OF YEARS, NOR IN THOUSANDS OF YEARS, BUT *IN ONLY ONE GENERATION.*" [1]

Did you get that?   In just one generation!

HOW IT WORKS

A child receives half its genes from each parent. Let's call these genes A and B. The genes have partners, a and b.

Genes A and B are good at producing melanin (which darkens the skin). Result: A person with two pairs of genes *AA and BB* will have *darker* skin.

Genes *a and b* both produce less melanin. Result: A person with two pairs of genes *aa and bb* will have *very light* skin.

A person with gene pairs *Aa and Bb* (let's write it as *AaBb*) will have *medium-coloured* skin.

And so on.

Now, *suppose both parents are AaBb* (medium-brown).

The mother gives the child two genes for skin colour – one from type A or a, the other from B or b. The father likewise gives two genes for skin colour – one from type A or a, the other from B or b.

So each of these middle-brown parents with *AaBb* can give his/her children any one of the following pairs of gene combinations: AB, Ab, aB or ab.

For example, suppose each parent passes on the AB combination to the new child. The mother gives the child *AB*. The father gives the child *AB*. Result: The child will be born with *AABB* – and thus will be *PURE BLACK*.

But if both parents pass on the ab combination (the mother giving the child *ab*; the father giving the child *ab*), then what? Result: The child will be born with *aabb* – and will be *PURE WHITE*.

… EVEN THOUGH BOTH PARENTS WERE MEDIUM-BROWN SKINNED!

HOW COLOUR BECOMES PERMANENT

Notice that the PURE BLACK child is born *AABB* – that is, he has *no genes for lightness*. If a group of pure black persons is isolated,

171

their offspring will be only black. These children will have *lost* the ability to be "white".

Likewise, when *aabb* children marry their own type (pure white) and move away to interbreed only among themselves, they will produce from now on only white offspring. They have lost their ability to be black. They no longer have genes to produce a great deal of melanin.

If we started today with just two MIDDLE-BROWN parents, they could produce extreme racial colours (BLACK and WHITE), in a way that races would have PERMANENTLY DIFFERENT colours.

A fixed middle-brown colour could also be produced. If the original middle-brown parents produce children of either *AAbb* or *aaBB* and these offspring move away and interact only with their kind, their descendants will be a fixed middle-brown colour.

REVERSING THE PROCESS

Despite marked differences, the races would disappear if total inter-marriage were practised today. There would reappear a brown coloured majority, with a sprinkling of every other shade permitted within the genetic pool.

The genes for Chinese almond eyes, black skin or white, etcetra, would still exist, but the combinations would be different.

Interestingly, you can find the characteristics of ANY race in EVERY race. For example, some Europeans have broad, flat noses, and others have short, frizzy hair, but on average Europeans do not have these features. The same sorts of genetic recombinations that have produced skin colour variations have produced other body variations – straight hair, wavy hair, eye shape, eye colour, body height, and so on.

We do not know the total number of gene differences which mark off a Negro from a white Dane. One authority considers it unlikely that there are more than six pairs of genes in which the white race differs characteristically from the black.[2]

GENES FOR ALL RACES
EXISTED AT THE START

The first man was designed with the best possible combination of skin-colour genes for his perfect created environment.

The Great Flood radically altered that environment.

Evidently, Noah's family possessed genes for both light and dark skin, dark enough to protect them, yet light enough to ensure sufficient Vitamin D.

ALL RACIAL VARIETIES COULD APPEAR IN JUST ONE GENERATION

From the above data it can be seen that all the known varieties of skin colour could come from one pair of mid-brown parents IN ONE GENERATION.

In general, racial characteristics are recombinations of pre-existing, created hereditary (genetic) information. They have not evolved and they do not require a long time to become apparent.

Let's be clear on this. There has been *no evolution of genes that did not previously exist.* All that has occurred is the *recombination* and degeneration of created genetic information.

The splitting up of a large group into many smaller groups who became isolated from each other would provide the ideal condition for the RAPID APPEARANCE of many different racial groups with distinct characteristics.

This is doubtless what occurred. There is overwhelming archaeological evidence for a common origin for *all* races on this planet.[3]

In Book 3 of this series, we shall touch on the fact of an original common language for the whole human race – and how a dispersion occurred from an area of the Middle East. The biblical account of this event (supported by many ancient traditions of nations everywhere) fits the evidence well.

The scattering of mankind shortly after the Great Flood, when their language was suddenly confused, was the catalyst that produced the variations now seen.

IT HAS *NOT* TAKEN COUNTLESS MILLENNIA TO PRODUCE THE DIFFERENCES WE SEE TODAY.

Before leaving this question, it may be of interest to note a comment by Professor William C. Boyd, Professor of Immunochemistry at the Boston University School of Medicine:

"We should not be surprised if identical genes crop up in all corners of the earth, or if the over-all racial differences we detect

173

prove to be small. We do not know the total number of gene differences which mark off a Negro of the Alur tribe in the Belgian Congo from a white native of Haderslev, Denmark. Glass has suggested that the number of gene differences even in such a case is probably small. Besides a few genes for skin colour, he thinks that there may be a dominant gene for kinky hair and a pair or two of genes for facial features. He considers it unlikely that there are *more than six pairs of genes* in which the white race differs *characteristically* from the black. This estimate errs somewhat on the small side, in the opinion of the present writer. Probably, however, it is of the right order of magnitude, and any outraged conviction that the difference between the two races must be much greater than this, which some persons might feel, is likely to be based on emotional, rather than rational, factors." [4]

The differences did *not* take countless ages to produce.

THE MANY NEW ANIMAL AND PLANT VARIETIES

But what about the numerous animal and plant species? Isn't time a problem, here?

Formation of so many varieties of animals and plants from each original type in the Ark – wouldn't this have required much longer time than just a few thousand years?

On the Galapagos Islands, for example, there are 13 species of finches. It is usually speculated that for these to develop from an original pair of finches must have taken from one million to five million years.

Well, let's see.

VARIATION WITHIN THE KIND

It is important, at this stage, to understand a basic fact of genetics.

The laws of genetics have shown us that each basic type, whether dog, butterfly or human, has programmed into it the capacity for variation. This ensures survival in different environments.

The Yarrow is an example of the marvellous adaptability which lies within the hereditary complex of many plant kinds:

- medium height races along the coast

174

-   tall races inland
-   low, mat-forming races on the mountain tops.

Yet, with all this variety within the basic type, there is never any doubt that a new race of yarrow is still a yarrow.

It is true, you see, that an organism's DNA programme (inbuilt set of instructions) imposes limits:
-   variations within the basic type, yes,
                    BUT
-   capacity to turn into a different basic type of organism, no!

Take dogs, for example. From an original pair have come wolves, dingoes, coyotes, and so on.

In the varieties that appear, *no new genetic information* is introduced. Each new variety is more *specialised* than the original parent, and thus carries less information – and consequently has less potential for further selection. (Thus, in dogs, you can't breed Great Danes from Chihuahuas.)

So no matter how many variations take place within a "kind", kangaroos are still kangaroos, dogs are still dogs and finches are still finches.

A long-legged sheep may mutate into a short-legged sheep – but never into a deer. A white moth species may change into a grey moth – but never will it become a spider. Scientific breeders can produce seedless grapefruit, white turkeys, cattle without horns – but all within the limits of the original type.

There are LIMITS to change, you see. These limits are set by the amount of information that was originally present, from which to select.

SPEED OF NEW SPECIES DEVELOPMENT
SINCE THE FLOOD

Now for the time factor.

Sweet peas can be frilled, plain, scented, scentless, red, white or blue – but they are still sweet peas. Did you know that of the 500 types of sweet pea we have, all have developed from a single type since the year 1700?

Well, that's artificial selection, someone will say. That is quick, because man is deliberately acting on each generation.

175

So let's observe natural selection at work on its own.

An intensive 18 year study of the Galapagos finches has been undertaken by Princeton zoology professor Peter Grant. He found that during years of drought, as finches depleted the small-seed supply, the finches that survived were those with larger, deeper beaks which could get at the remaining large seeds. This shifted the population in that direction.

Grant was amazed at the *observed* rate of change in the population. At this *observed* rate, he estimates, it would take only 1,200 years to transform the medium ground finch into the cactus finch, for example. Or only 200 years to convert it into the more similar large ground finch.[5]

Remember, however, that *no new genes are being produced* by mutation. It is simply the selection of what is already there. This fails to qualify as evidence for real, uphill (macro) evolution.

Rather, it is evidence that "downhill" adaptation into several varieties can easily occur *in just a few centuries* – not requiring millions of years.

Bear in mind, also, that after the Flood, with residual catastrophes occurring as the earth was settling down and drying out (see Book 3 of this series), with changing climate, and rapid migration into new, empty niches, selection pressure would have been much more intense.

The time factor since the Great Flood is quite adequate, you see.

EPILOGUE

What, then, have we discovered?

PHYSICAL EVIDENCE
There is solid, tangible evidence that:

1. A disaster of extraordinary proportions has occurred on this planet.
2. It was sudden.
3. Life forms worldwide were rapidly buried in sediments laid down by moving water. (This is fully consistent with a global Flood.)
4. It involved human beings.
5. These victims were highly civilised.

TRADITIONS
Virtually all of ancient mankind said they "remembered" such an event. Obviously, the disaster must have had some degree of reality to be so deeply entwined in the histories of so many cultures.

The skeptic should now ask himself: Is there *good reason* why we should not credit these reports?

After all, the reports do tally with the facts - remains that can be seen and touched today. These cannot be argued away.

IN BOOK 2 OF THIS 3-PART SERIES, WE SHALL UNCOVER THESE STARTLING PHYSICAL RELICS.

A ONCE PERFECT CLIMATE
The former world was rich beyond our dreams - in its stark beauty, in its environment and its quality of life. On that, physical evidence and historical traditions agree. It appears that the world then was as perfect as one could desire. Everything about it was just right.

Mankind, so the sacred records affirm, was placed on this beautiful planet as its custodian. He was granted every privilege, including a free will to make his own decisions.

But something went wrong. Deadly wrong.

WHY… WHY… WHY?

I recall Hank's words, that first day we had met in the backpacker lodge.

"He's got some questions to answer… if he exists," challenged Hank. "If God made this world good, as that old Book says, then:

- Why is the climate so HARSH?
- Why the hurricanes, floods and droughts that destroy so much life?
- Why is only 18 percent of our world suitable for human habitation? Why are huge areas under desert or under perpetual ice?
- Why is the soil impoverished, so that millions starve?
- WHAT KIND OF GOD WOULD CREATE THIS KIND OF WORLD???"

If a Superior Intelligence – a Supreme Being – did make this place, then, as we've now seen, He did hand over to us a mighty fine planet to start with. With freedom to enjoy it.

So what went wrong?

Well, we do make our own choices. And you can trust *US* to mess things up!

So is it fair to blame someone else?

Oh well, that's another story.

APPENDIX

The Bird in the Desert

On December 29, 1946, the American zoologist Edmund Jager and a party of students were on an expedition in the Mojave Desert of southern California.

As the group passed through a small, narrow canyon in the Chuckawalla Mountains, Jager spotted something curious on the wall of a cliff. In one of the numerous weathered shallow hollows no bigger than a hand, sat a bird. It was a poor-will. Its spotted grey plumage harmonised perfectly with the crystalline structure of the grey granite.

They paused to watch it for about ten minutes. The bird gave not the slightest sign of life. Then Jager stretched out his hand to touch it. He ran his hand down its back several times, but the bird gave no reaction to suggest that there was any life left in it.

The group trudged on. About two hours later, when they came back through the small canyon again, there was the bird, still sitting in the hollow. Its position was unchanged.

This time Jager reached in and took the bird out. It felt unusually light. In fact, it seemed to be dried out. The bird's feet and its eyelids, on which a bird's temperature can be felt, were plain cold. Jager concluded that the bird had frozen to death in its place of shelter. He placed the poor-will back in the hollow, then they continued their trek.

Jager mentioned the incident to his friend, Professor Lloyd Smith, who expressed an interest to see this unusual find.

So ten days after his first visit, Jager was back with his friend – and there was the bird, still in the same place, its position unchanged.

One of the men removed it from the niche. Then, as he was holding it to examine it, an amazing thing happened. The poor-will's beak opened, and the bird uttered a few very high-pitched, whimpering, squeaking notes.

And the poor-will's eyes opened briefly – or so they both thought. Then suddenly the bird lifted its wings. But the movement looked lifeless and mechanical.

Cautiously, Jager attempted to fold the wings back into their previous position, but he couldn't. As soon as he let go, the wings just snapped back, like steel springs, into the lifted position. So he used force, and succeeded finally to lay them flat against the body.

Then Jager placed the bird back into its hollow to remain there as an oddity - something to show future student expeditions. The bird did not look so good after all the handling. The plumage was now tousled and the wings stood at an unnatural angle.

The two scientists went on through the canyon. Passing back two hours later, they saw that nothing had changed. The bird remained in the same unnatural posture into which they had placed it earlier.

However, they thought this would make an interesting camera shot, so they again took the bird from its niche to hold it.

Then something happened that startled them. The poor-will suddenly flew up and away.

The men could hardly believe their eyes. They just stood there watching, as the bird, wings beating rapidly, flew skilfully up along the cliff wall and found itself another rock hollow higher up beyond their reach.

How ever could this be? Had they been witnessing a bird in hibernation, which had been progressively awakened or disturbed by their handling, and had finally had flown away?

We know that during hibernation, the metabolism of animals is sharply reduced. Observations of mammals in hibernation have confirmed that the normal rate of 300 heartbeats a minute declines to just 5 beats. An animal in hibernation has only its pilot light going, so to speak.

But until this incident, hibernation in birds had never been observed.

Almost a year later, at the end of November 1947, Jager came back. And he was fortunate to find the poor-will again, in the very same cliff niche.

On this occasion, he had the opportunity to conduct careful studies. He was able to confirm that a bird – and a desert bird at that - could indeed hibernate.

First, he took the bird's temperature at the anus. The reading was 18 degrees C. (that is 64 degrees F). Since that was higher than the temperature of the surroundings, it proved that the bird was still alive and was actually in hibernation. The normal temperature of this bird is about 42 degrees C. (108 degrees F.), so the poor-will had lowered its body temperature by about 24 degrees C. (44 degrees F).

When the scientist applied a stethoscope to the bird's breast it told him nothing. The poor-will's heart was beating so slowly and feebly that it could not be heard.

He then placed a cold metal mirror in front of the bird's nostrils. The mirror did not mist over, as would be the case if there was any noticeable breathing.

To determine once and for all if the bird was alive, Jager tried a final experiment. Opening one of the creature's eyelids, he flashed a penlight into the pupil of the eye. Again, he observed no reaction. In fact, the bird did not even try to close its eyelid.

But the bird was definitely alive, The measured body temperature proved that.

Every two weeks Jager came back to weigh the bird. The weight was found to be slowly diminishing: 45.61 grams, 45.58 grams, 45.50 grams, 44.56 grams.

These measurements indicated the very slow rate at which the hibernating bird was consuming its reserves of fat. The hibernation continued right through winter – for three months. Then the bird ended its deathlike rigidity, having consumed only 6 grams of fat.

Interestingly, this bird came back to hibernate in the very same hollow in that same cliff for the next two years, 1948 and 1949.

In response to his published report, Jager received many letters reporting similar phenomena.

NOTES

PREFACE

1 *Dead Men's Secrets*, page 349

2 Details appear in Book 3 of this series, *The Corpse Came Back.*

Chapter 1 – CITY UNDER THE SEA

1 M. Ewing, "New Discoveries on the Mid-Atlantic Ridge," *National Geographic Magazine*, Vol. XCVI, No.5 - Nov. 1949

2 Otto Muck, *The Secret of Atlantis*, p.146

Chapter 2 – ANTARCTICA'S PALM BEACHES

1 D.G. Whitley, "The Ivory Islands in the Arctic Ocean", *Journal of the Philosophical Society of Great Britain*, XII, 1910, p.49. Cited in *Earth in Upheaval*, by Immanuel Velikovsky, Dell ed., 1955, p.19

2 George McCready Price, *The New Geology*. Mountain View, Calif.: Pacific Press Publishing Association, 1923, p.654

3 Alfred Russell Wallace, *The Geographical Distribution of Animals*, Vol 1. New York: Harper and Brothers, 1876, p. 277

4 Sir William Dawson, geologist, cited by Samuel Kinns, *Moses and Geology*. London: Cassell and Company, 1886, p.166

5 R.W. Chaney, *Bulletin of the Geological Society of America*, 51 : 469-488. *Scientific Monthly*, 51 : 489-499

6 pp.243-245

7 O.D. von Engeln and Kenneth E. Caster, *Geology*.   New York: McGraw-Hill Book Co., Inc., 1952, p.491. Whitcomb and Morris, pp.250-255

8 Harold T. Wilkins, *Mysteries of Ancient South America*. Secaucus, N.J.: Citadel Press, 1974, p.30

9   E.H. Colbert, "Evolutionary Growth Rates in the Dinosaurs", *Scientific Monthly*, August 1949, p.71

10 *Genesis 1:9,10*

11 *Genesis 2:10-14*

12 *ch. 2:5-6*

13 *Genesis 1:31*

Chapter 3 – THE WEATHER MAN WHO GOT IT WRONG!

1   *Genesis 1:7*

2   Adelaide *News*, Jan. 12, 1970

3   *Hebrews 11:7*

Chapter 4 – LOBSTER AS BIG AS A MAN

1   Wallace, *The Geographical Distribution of Animals*, Vol. I. New York: Harper and Brothers, 1876, p.150,151

2   Sir Henry Howarth, *The Mammoth and the Flood.* London: Sampson, Low, Marston, Searle and Risington, 1887, p.351

3   *Genesis 6:4*

Chapter 5 – IF A SNAKE BITES YOU...

1   Baugh and Wilson, *Dinosaur*, pp.140-145

2   *Genesis 1:7,8*

3   Carl E. Baugh, *Panorama of Creation*. Fort Worth, Texas: Creation Publication services, 1992, pp.47-48

4   *Ibid.,* p.48

5   *Ibid.*, p.57

6   Gilmore, Elaine, "Sunflower over Tokyo," *Popular Science*, May 1988, p. 75

7   Hiroshi, Koichibara, "Tomatomation," *UNESCO Courier*, March 1987

Chapter 6 – ANCIENT NUCLEAR REACTOR

1   *Revelation 21:18*

2   Roman Black, *Old and New Australian Aboriginal Art*, "The Story of the Boomerang"

3   Carl E. Baugh, *Panorama of Creation*, p.66

Chapter 7 – COULD YOU REALLY LIVE TO BE 600?

1   A.M. Rehwinkel, *The Flood*.   Saint Louis, Missouri : Concordia Publishing House, 1951, p.140

2   Josephus, *Antiquities of the Jews*

3   Alan and Sally Landsburg, *The Outer Space Connection*. London: Transworld Publishers, Ltd., 1975, p.148, emphasis added

4   *Ibid*, p.148

5   *Ibid*, p.121

6   *Ibid.*, p.121

7   Hans Selys, "Is Ageing Curable?"   *Science Digest*, Vol.46, December 1959, p.1

8   Andrew Tomas, *We Are Not the First*. London: Sphere, 1971

9   R. Young, *Analytical Concordance of the Bible*, 8th ed. Lutterworth Press, Guildford and London, 1977

10   *Genesis 1:29,30; 3:18; 9:2-5*

11   Gilbert N. Plass, "Carbon Dioxide and Climate," *Scientific*

American, Variation of Lease.201, July 1959, p.42

12 *Genesis 6:3; 9:3-5*

13 *New Woman*, Feb. 1993, pp.88-90

14. *Genesis 1:29-30*

15 *Reviewing* the book by Chris Rucker and Jan Hoffman, *The Seventh-day Diet* (Random House), 1991

16 Chris Rucker in an interview with the U.S. magazine *Bottom Line,* 1991

Chapter 8 – JUDGMENT DAY

1 Rene Noorbergen, *The Ark File* Mountain View, Ca.: Pacific Press Publishing Association, 1974, p.56

2 Francis Hitching, *World Atlas of Mysteries.* London: Pan Books, Ltd., 1978, p.165

3 *Genesis 6:1*

4 *Genesis.6:5*

5 *Genesis 6:12*

6 *Genesis.6:11*

7 Jonathan Eisen, *Suppressed Inventions and Other Discoveries.* New York: Avery publishing Group, 1999, p.504

Chapter 9 – WORLD IN SHOCK

1 Tim La Haye and John Morris, *The Ark on Ararat*, pp.233-238

2 Hugh Miller, *The Testimony of the Rocks.* New York: John B. Alden, 1892

3 Ibid, p.284

4 Violet Cummings, *Has Anyone Really Seen Noah's Ark*? San Diego,

Calif.: Creation-Life Publishers, 1982, p.233

5   *Genesis.6:5-7,13*

6   *Genesis.6:13-18; 7:13*

7   *Genesis.6:14-16; 7:13*

8   H.H. Bancroft, *Works of Bancroft, Native Races*. San Francisco: A.L. Bancroft and Company, 1883, vol.V, pp.20,21

9   *De Dea Syria*, sec.12

10   The *Bhagawata Purana*, a Hindu poem of great antiquity (*Asiatic Researches*, vol.ii, mem.7

11   *Gen.7:11*

12   *Genesis 7:13*

13   Harold T. Wilkins, *Secret Cities of Old South America*, p. 419

14   C.H. Kang and Ethel R. Nelson, *The Discovery of Genesis*. St. Louis: Concordia Publishing House, 1979

15   Genesis 7:13

16   *Genesis 7:11*

17   D. Davidson and H. Aldersmith, *The Great Pyramid: Its Divine Message*. London: Williams and Norgate, Ltd., 1936, p.38

18   *Ibid.*, p.25

19   John Urquhart, *Modern Discoveries and the Bible*. London: Marshall Brothers, 1898, pp.175ff

20   *Dead Men's Secrets*

21   pp.438ff

22   Harold T. Wilkins, *Mysteries of Ancient South America*. Secaucus, N.J.: Citadel Press, 1974, p.31

23   The *Harris Papyrus*; the *Hermitage Papyrus*; the *Ipuwer Papyrus*

24   *Genesis 7:11*

25   *Genesis 7:19,20*

26   Alfred M. Rehwinkel, *The Flood*. St.Louis, Mo.: Concordia Publishing House, 1951, pp.131,132

186

27 Charles Berlitz, *Mystery of Atlantis*. St. Albans, U.K.: Panther Books, Ltd., 1979, pp.45-48

28 J.Legge , tr. "Annals of the Bamboo Books", vol. 3, part 1, of *The Chinese Classics*. Hong Kong, 1876

29 *Genesis 7:11; 8:13,14*

30 *Genesis 8:5-12*

31 Rehwinkel, p.135

32 *Genesis 9:13-15*

33 Mayan *Book of Chilam Balam of Chumayel*

Chapter 10 – A CANNIBAL'S TALE

1 William Wundt, *Elements of Folk Psychology*. New York: Macmillan Company, 1916, p.392

2 See Jonathan Gray's *Update International*, No. 7, p.15

3 Gray, private files

4 David Fasold, *The Discovery of Noah's Ark*. U.K.: Sidgwick and Jackson Ltd., 1990, pp.16,17, 194,195. E.A. Wallis Budge, *The Egyptian Book of the Dead*

5 *Genesis 8:4*

6 *W.F. Albright, Yahweh and the Gods of Canaan. London: Athlone Press, 1968, p.86. See also: Clifford Wilson, Crash Go the Chariots. New York: Lancer Books, 1972, pp.45-51. Wilson, The Chariots Still Crash. Old Tappan, N.J.: Fleming H. Revell and Co., 1976, pp.129-140*

7 *Kenneth A. Kitchen, Ancient Orient and the Old Testament, p.89*

8 *Tim La Haye and John Morris, The Ark on Ararat, pp.232,233*

9 *Alexander Heidel, The Gilgamesh Epic and Old Testament, pp.224-258*

Chapter 11 – THE FLOOD THAT NEVER REALLY WENT AWAY

1   *Genesis 6:17 – 8:22*

2   *Genesis 7:19*

3   *Genesis 7:24; 8:13; - compare 7:11*

4   *Genesis 6:5-7, 11-13*

5   *Genesis 6:17,18; 7:23; 9:19; 1 Peter 3:20; 2 Peter 2:5; Luke 17:27*

6   *Genesis 6:13*

7   *2 Peter 3:6*

8   *Genesis 9:11,15*

9   See the third book in this series of three, *The Corpse Came Back.*

10 See an article by Lt. Col. Davies, in *Journal of Transactions of the Victoria Institute.* London, 1930, p.95

11 *Genesis 7:11*

12 Francis Hitching, *World Atlas of Mysteries.* London: Pan Books, Ltd., 1978, p.95

13 *World Book of Science.* Year 1987, art. "The World's Deepest Well", pp.206-207

Chapter 12 – WHY HANK GASPED

1   "Evolution's erratic pace", *Natural History*, Vol. LXXXVI – 5- May 1977, p.14

2   Andrew Snelling, B.Sc. (Hons), Ph.D. (Geology) and Steven Austin, B.S., M.S., Ph.D. (geology), in "Startling Evidence for Noah's Flood.", *Creation Ex Nihilo*, vol.15, no.1, Dec.1992-Feb.1993, pp.47-50

3   Sylvia Baker, M.Sc., *Bone of Contention.* Sunnybank, Queensland, Australia: Creation Science Foundation Ltd., 1986, p.32

Chapter 13 – NO ROOM FOR ERROR

1   *Genesis 6:15-16*

2   Jonathan Gray, *The Ark Conspiracy, 1993, ch. 8.* - http:www.archaeologyanswers.com/tac.html

3   *Principles of Systematic Zoology.* New York: McGraw-Hill, 1969, pp.11,12

4   Barry Fell, *America B.C.* London: Wildwood House Ltd., 1978, p.110

5   Jonathan Gray, *Dead Men's Secrets*, pp.78,79 – http://www.archaeologyanswers.com

6   *Encyclopaedia Brittanica*, art.: "Ship Design and Construction", Vol.16, p.689. 1982

7   Nelson C. Brown, *Encyclopedia Americana*, art.: "Wood", Vol.29, p.116, 1983

8   See our book *Dead Men's Secrets, p.10.*

9   *Genesis 4:22, The Living Bible.* London: Coverdale House Publishers, 1974

10 Violet Cummings, *Has Anyone Really Seen Noah's Ark?* San Diego, Calif.: Creation-Life Publishers, 1982, p.224

11 Rene Noorbergen, *The Ark File*, pp.74-75. Mountain View, California: Pacific Press Publishing Association, 1974

12 W.P. Pycraft, *Encyclopaedia Brittanica*, art. "Hibernation", 1956, p.539

13 Marston Bates, "Hibernation", article in *Collier's Encyclopedia*, 1956, Vol. 7, p.11

14 *Psalm 29:10*

Chapter 14 – DATING SHOCK

1   This pressure dependence was reported in 1973 in *Science*, vol.181,

no.4104, pp.1164-65

2   Frederic B. Jueneman, FAIC, "Secular Catastrophism", *Industrial Research and Development*, June, 1982, p.21

3   Henry Faul, *Nuclear Geology*. New York: John Wiley and Sons, Inc., 1954, p.297

4   M.A. Cook, *Prehistory and Earth Models*. London: Max Parrish and Co., Ltd., 1960, pp.53-60

5   M.R. Klepper and D.G. Wyant, "Notes on the Geology of Uranium", *U.S. Geological Survey Bulletin*. 1046-F, 1957, p.93

6   W.D. Stansfield, Instructor of Biology, California Polytech State University, *The Science of Evolution*. New York: Macmillan and Co., 1977, pp.82,84

7   M.L. Keith and G.M. Anderson, Department of Geochemistry and Mineralogy, Pennsylvania State University, "Radiocarbon Dating: Fictitious Results With Mollusc Shells", *Science*, vol.141, 16 August, 1963, pp.634-635

8   Wakefield Dort, Jnr., Department of Geology, The University of Kansas, "Mummified Seals of Southern Victoria Land", *Antarctic Journal* (Washington), vol.6, September-October, 1971, p.211

9   Dr. Alan C. Riggs - formerly of the U.S. Geological Survey, now on the staff of the University of Washington, Seattle, "Major Carbon-14 Deficiency in Modern Snail Shells From Southern Nevada Springs", *Science*, vol.224, 6 April, 1984, p.58

10. R. Matthews, *Ex Nihilo*, Queensland, Australia, vol.5,no.1, 1982, 9.41

11 Faul, *Nuclear Geology*. New York: Wiley and Sons, Inc., 1954; *Ages of Rocks, Planets and Stars*. McGraw-Hill, 1966. R. Russel and R. Farquhar, *Lead Isotopes in Geology*. New York: Interscience Publishing, 1960

12 Joel W. Grossman, *1987 Brittanica Book of the Year*. Chicago: Encyclopaedia Brittanica, Inc., 1987, pp.143-144, art.:Archaeology

13 *Nature Physical Science*, vol.232, 19 July, 1971, pp.60-61

14 *Science*, vol.162, p.265. *Journal of Geophysical Research*, vol.73,

p.4601. *American Journal of Science*, vol.262, p.154

15 *World Archaeology*, vol.7, 1975, p.160

16 *Science*, vol.213, 28 August, 1981, p.1003

17 *Science*, vol.220, 17 June, 1983, p.1271

18 N. Jones, "Did Blast From Below Destroy Tunguska?", *New Scientist*, p. 14, September 7, 2002

19 Richard L. Mauger -Associate Professor of Geology, East Carolina University, "K-Ar Ages of Biotites From Tuffs in Eocene Rocks of the Green River, Washakie, and Uinta Basins, Utah, Wyoming, and Colorado", *Contributions to Geology, University of Wyoming*, vol.15- 1, 1977, p.37

20 E.H. Andrews, Professor of Materials, University of London, and Head of the Department of Materials at Queen Mary College, in book, *God, Science and Evolution*"

21 Robert E. Lee, "Radiocarbon: Ages in Error" *Anthropological Journal of Canada*, vol.19-3, 1981, pp.9-29

22 T. Save-Soderbergh and I.U. Olsson -Institute of Egyptology and Institute of Physics respectively, University of Uppsala, Sweden, "C14 Dating and Egyptian Chronology," in *Radiocarbon Variations and Absolute Chronology, Proceedings of the Twelfth Nobel Symposium*, Ingrid U. Olsson – ed,, Almqvist and Wiksell, Stockholm, and John Wiley and Sons, Inc., New York, 1970, p.35

23 George Howe, *Carbon 14 and Other Radio-Active Dating Methods*, p.11

24 C. Patterson, G. Tilton and M. Inghram, *Science*, vol.121, 1955, p.69

25 "Creation in the Physics Lab." -Interview with Dr. D. Russell Humphries, by Dr. Carl Wieland, *Creation Ex Nihilo*, vol.15, no.3, June-August, 1993, p.23

Chapter 15 – THE COVER-UP

1 Melvin A. Cook, "Do Radiological Clocks Need Repair?" *Creation Research Society Quarterly*, vol.5, October, 1968, p.70

2   T. Norman and B. Setterfield, *The Atomic Constants, Light and Time*, August, 1987. Stanford Research Institute; Professor V.S. Troitskii, article in *Astrophysics and Space Science*, Vol. 139, pp.389-411, December, 1987

3   "How Old is the Earth?", *The FCM Informer*, January/February 2001, p.23

4.   Sigurdur Thorarinsson, *Surtsey*. Almenna, Reykjavik, Iceland, 1964

5   H. Blatt, G. Middleton and R. Murray, *Origin of Sedimentary Rocks*. Prentice-Hall, 1972, p.410

6   *Earth and Planetary Science Letters*, April, 1989

7   *Creation Ex Nihilo*, vol.15, no.3, June-August, 1993, pp.21,22

8   J.H. Hall and P.T. Robinson, "Deep Crustal Drilling in the North Atlantic Ocean", *Science*, vol. 204, May 11, 1979, p. 578

9   Brian Sykes, *Nature*, vol.352, August 1, 1991, p.381

10   *New Scientist*, October 17, 1992, p.15

11   *New Scientist*, October 31, 1992, p.18 ; *Creation Ex Nihilo*, vol.15, no.2, March-May, 1993, p.9

12   It took 20 years for scientists to accept that these were dinosaur bones. An initial announcement was printed in 1985 in *Geological Society of America abstract programs* vol.17, p.548. Already in press at that time was an article describing the site and the condition of the bones: Kyle L. Davies, "Duckbill Dinosaurs [Hadrosauridae, Ornithischia] from the North Slope of Alaska", *Journal of Paleontology*, vol.61, no.1, pp.198-200

13   *Creation Ex Nihilo*, vol.14, no.3, June-August, 1992, pp.16-17

14   M. Schweitzer and T. Staedter, 'The Real Jurassic Park', *Earth* , June 1997 pp. 55-57

Chapter 16 – NOT ENOUGH TIME?

1   John Mackay, *Ex Nihilo*, vol.6, no.4, May, 1984. Emphasis added

2   William C. Boyd (Professor of Immunochemistry at Boston School

of Medicine), *Genetics and the Races of Man.* P.200ff

3   Jonathan Gray, *Dead Men's Secrets,* pp.16-19. http:www.archaeologyanswers.com

4   William C. Boyd, *Genetics and the Races of Man*, p. 200f.

5   P.R. Grant, "Natural Selection and Darwin's Finches", *Scientific American*, October, 1991, pp.60-65

INDEX

Aborigines 53,84,87,88,95,145,170
Antarctic 22-24,30,161-162
Antedeluvian world
- atmosphere 43-49,56
- civilization 76-77
- climate 23-27,31,34-35,54-56,66
- corruption 77-78
- flora and fauna 13,30
- gigantism 36-43
- intelligence 75-76
- land area 15,28
- longevity 35,57-58
- mountains 27
- no rain 29-30,31,34
- ocean 17-19,27
- population 72-74
- radiation free 65-66
- soil fertility 64-65
- ten generations 70-71
- thermonuclear reactor   54-56
- water canopy 32-35,46-49,66,117
Ark
- legends of 84
- scientific questions on 126-142
Atlantis 70
Atmosphere
- age of 152
- pre-Flood 43-49,56

Babylonian
- Flood tradition 102-105
- "king" list 71-72
Beaches, rapidly formed 159
Biblical version superior 102-105
Blood cells in dinosaurs 166-168

-   of the Flood 82-106
Light, speed of 156
Longevity 35,57-58

Magnetic reversals 163-164
Magnetic field 158-159
Moon 157
Mountains covered 111,119-120

Natural selection 173-175
Noah's Ark 126-142
Nuclear heating 54-56

Ocean
-   age of 158
-   pre-Flood 17-19,27
Oil 161

Population, 72-74
Pre-Flood world, See Antedeluvian world
Prophecy 78,140-142

Races, origin of 169-176
Radiometric dating, See Dating methods
Rain, none pre-Flood 29-30,31,34

Sea, pre-Flood 19-17,27
Sea level risen 17-19
Shorelines, formed rapidly 159
Snake venom 44
Species development, speed of 173-176
Stalactites 160
Stars 53-54
St. Helens, Mount 162-163
Strata 119-121,163
Sudden
-   dropping of ocean bed 18
-   burial of fossils 120

We invite you to view the complete
selection of titles we publish at:

www.LNFBooks.com

or write or email us your praises,
reactions, or thoughts about this
or any other book we publish at:

TEACH Services, Inc.
P.O. Box 954
Ringgold, GA 30736

info@TEACHServices.com

www.ingramcontent.com/pod-product-compliance
Lightning Source LLC
Chambersburg PA
CBHW071121280326
41935CB00010B/1080